HOW TO RAISE FU

HOW TO RAISE FUNDS AND SPONSORSHIP

In this Series

RAISE FUNDS & SPONSORSHIP

A Complete Step-by-Step Guide to Success

Chriss McCallum

How To Books

By the same author

How to Write for Publication

British Library cataloguing-in-publication data
A catalogue record for this book is available
from the British Library.

© 1992 by Chriss McCallum

Cartoons by Mike Flanagan

First published in 1992 by How To Books Ltd, Plymbridge House, Estover
Road, Plymouth PL6 7PZ, United Kingdom. Tel: Plymouth (0752)
735251/695745 Fax: (0752) 695699. Telex: 45635.

Typeset by Concept Communications Ltd, Crayford, Kent.
Printed and bound in Great Britain by
Dotesios Ltd, Trowbridge, Wiltshire.

Contents

List of illustrations

Preface

Your project might be modest, or it might be ambitious. Your target might be £1,000 or £1,000,000. Whatever your goal, your strategy for raising money for charity needs to be thoroughly thought out, planned and organised.

Consider this: approximately every half-hour a new appeal joins the tens of thousands in the United Kingdom which are already competing for every penny they can draw from official sources and coax from the public.

More charitable appeals founder because they're launched 'half-baked' than for any other reason. Someone sees an urgent need or has a brilliant idea, the adrenalin begins to pump and they rush straight into action, impatient to get things moving. Please resist this impulse. High hopes, good intentions and hard work are not enough. You need planning, preparation, organisation and coordination.

This book shows you how to plan your fund-raising strategy, how to prepare your activities, where to look for donations, grants, sponsorship and practical help, and where to get all the advice and information you're likely to need.

It also gives the 'know-how' on organising successful fund-raising events and on running a charity shop, with detailed advice from experienced people.

Take whatever time is necessary to work out the strategies that are right for your cause, keep your supporters in the picture about what you're planning and how you'll be doing it, and you'll be on the road to success from the start.

Success generates success . . . its magnetism attracts people, because they like to be associated with it. And the more people who support your cause, the more successful you'll be.

Good luck.

Note: to avoid unnecessary repetition, details of addresses, prices, sources,

9

and so on of organisations, services, books, magazines and leaflets mentioned in the book are listed in the appendices.

All books refereed to in the text are available from bookshops or direct from the publishers. You should also be able to find any book currently in print in the UK in public libraries. If your local library doesn't have a copy in stock, they should be able to get one for you either from another branch in your area or through the Inter-Library Loan Service, for which there's usually a small charge.

1
Setting Up

Fund-raising these days is a challenge. There are no easy options. Fund-raisers who recognise the need for a well organised approach and strategy are far more likely to succeed than those who rely on haphazard methods and public generosity. Whether your group is new or already established, efficient cost-effective use of resources is vital.

Charitable organisations are learning very quickly that they must adopt businesslike attitudes. The *Directory of Social Change*, for example, has set up CharityFair 1992, the country's first 'trade' fair for charities. There was a time when such an event would have raised scandalised eyebrows in many a village hall. Not any more. The days of genteel, semi-apologetic approaches to raising money are long gone. That doesn't mean you have to be hard-hearted — just hard-headed.

You'll find it useful to keep in mind the key elements of successful fund-raising:

● clear identification of your cause
● leadership and organisation of personnel
● your overall strategy and timetable
● advance preparation
● 'marketing' your cause
● establishing trust and confidence between donors and cause.

We'll look at these elements in the pages that follow, and also at the range of possible sources of funding. Some of these will be more appropriate than others for your particular cause — the important thing is to know what is there, and to make sure that you neither overlook nor disregard *any* potential source of funds. We'll look at all the following possibilities:

● grants from central government
● grants from Europe

- grants from local authorities
- covenants, legacies and gifts
- grant-making trusts
- help from industry and commerce
- help from established fund-raising organisations
- local fund-raising events
- local and national radio appeals
- national TV appeals
- newspaper publicity
- media advertising
- raffles, lotteries and street collections
- charity shops
- car boot sales and market stalls
- events run by your own organisation and its supporters.

It's quite a list, isn't it? And you might be able to add more from your own experience and local knowledge. One possibility leads to another, and then another. . . Don't dismiss any idea until you've investigated it; thoroughness is a vital component of any successful enterprise.

IDENTIFYING YOUR CAUSE

Your first move is to identify your cause. What has brought this group of people together? What do you hope to achieve?

It's important to discuss this fully, so that you can produce a statement that clearly defines what the money you raise will be used for. Don't assume that everyone who comes along to your early meetings will be thinking along exactly the same lines. People put different interpretations on what they hear, and might be expecting something quite unlike what you're actually planning. The statement defining your aims and objectives should be agreed by everyone involved at the start, and should be put in writing before you allocate jobs and begin to plan your fund-raising. A clear and precisely focused purpose will avoid future problems because:

- Everyone concerned will know exactly what they're working for, and anyone who has doubts can withdraw before either your time or theirs is wasted.

- There's less danger of people working at cross purposes and possibly hampering progress or even damaging your cause.

- You'll be able to establish an unambiguous and easily recognisable identity, essential in dealing with the public.

- You can agree and allocate key positions in your organisation with confidence in your personnel.

DRAFTING YOUR CONSTITUTION

Your constitution is the set of rules which will govern your activities and by which everyone who joins your organisation agrees to abide. This needn't be a long or complicated document, but you do need to have your rules on paper in case of future misunderstandings or disagreements. Also, if you want to apply for registration as a charity you'll be required to submit a detailed constitution to the Charity Commission, in which case it's advisable to have the document drawn up (or at least checked) by a solicitor.

The exact form and content will depend on what kind of organisation you want to set up and how you want to run it (see Chapter 2, Charitable Status), but normally you should include the following clauses:

1. **Name:** The name by which your organisation will be known.

2. **Objects:** The purpose for which your organisation has been created.

3. **Powers:** The ways and means by which the organisation will pursue its objects.

4. **Trustees:** These are the people who govern the organisation. This clause sets out how they will be elected and discharged, and what the scope of their authority will be. (Charity Commission leaflet CC3 explains this in detail.)

5. **Power to amend the constitution:** This allows the Trustees to make any changes to the constitution that might become necessary over time, but normally the Trustees cannot be given power to alter the Objects clause of a registered charity.

6. **Management of funds:** This sets out the organisation's arrangements for looking after the money raised, including banking and, if appropriate, investment of funds.

7. **Annual accounts:** A registered charity is required to produce audited accounts annually. (It's advisable for an unregistered group to do so too, so that everyone involved — and the public if necessary — can see that all financial transactions are above board.)

8. **Dissolution:** This sets out what will happen to the organisation's assets if the group decides to wind up.

ETHICAL GUIDELINES

In these environmentally conscious times, you might want to draft a set of ethical guidelines in addition to your formal constitution. This is not a legal requirement, but it could be useful both in promoting your cause and in drawing up your list of possible funding sources. To give you an example, here are the ethical guidelines of the environmental charity Friends of the Earth, as drawn up in 1990 (they are subject to change from time to time):

'Friends of the Earth believes that fund-raising and sponsorship from industry and commerce is a legitimate part of the organisation's overall fund-raising strategy. This policy, however, must not undermine the integrity, credibility and independence of Friends of the Earth.

Friends of the Earth, therefore, will not accept donations, commercial sponsorship or product endorsement from:

● Any company which Friends of the Earth is actively campaigning against or contemplating a campaign against.

● Any company which has been the subject of any specific, sustained criticism in the organisation's campaigning materials.

● Any company causing indisputable, serious and avoidable damage to the environment.

● Any company which has been the target of any major or sustained local or national campaigns by other environmental organisations which might bring Friends of the Earth into conflict with those organisations.

● Any company which has been profiled as a target for campaigns by other sympathetic organisations.'

(Reproduced by permission of Friends of the Earth)

PERSONNEL

Before you get down to work, you'll probably want to set up at least a small **committee,** so that the workload can be shared equably. (Some people say that the most successful committee is a committee of one. This does avoid disagreements, but it takes an exceptionally energetic, organised and decisive person to keep all the necessary balls in the air.)

How many people does it take for a committee to function efficiently? Too few might find the workload over-demanding; too many might get bogged down in unnecessary debates over trivial issues. Only experience will show whether you've got the balance right, so don't tie your committee to long periods of service; you might need a 'cabinet shuffle' or two in the early weeks.

The duties and responsibilities attached to each job need to be defined *before* anyone takes it on, so there are no misunderstandings about who should be doing what. Take care not to let anyone take on a job that is obviously not right for them. There's no point in having a secretary who can't use a keyboard or a treasurer who can't cope with basic mathematics. It's usually a bad move, too, to give someone a job they don't really want but offer to do 'because nobody else wants to do it'. You need whole-hearted commitment, not self-sacrifice or martyrdom. These are early days, and as word of your project begins to spread, new volunteers might produce just the right person for that job.

Secondees

If you become a registered charity, or are operating under the umbrella of a registered charity, you might be able to get professional help free of charge in the form of a secondee assigned on a temporary or part-time basis by a local business. Many businesses in the UK provide this kind of practical help (see Chapter 5, Help from Industry and Commerce).

REACH

As a registered charity, you might also be able to get practical help from REACH, the Retired Executive Action Clearing-House. This organisation's membership is growing steadily, and there might be a member living in your area who could lend welcome expertise to your efforts. Keith Galpin, REACH's Development Manager, explains the organisation:

'As money for community and other charitable projects becomes harder to find, it's even more important that scarce funds are spent cost-effectively.

This means charities, however unworldly the cause, must adopt a hard-nosed and professional approach to the running of their own organisations.

Finding, and affording, the necessary expertise can be a problem. Commitment, hard work and dedication alone do not necessarily produce efficiency.

Fortunately, there is a growing group of highly qualified retired men and women, many still in their fifties or early sixties, who have the time and inclination to apply their career skills to help others — free!

Working for just one or two days each week, unpaid apart from expenses, these "retired" people are finding a new satisfaction and purpose in life. The organisations they work for range from giant national networks like Oxfam or the British Red Cross Society, to small, local groups struggling to become established.

REACH is the national charity which recruits these experts and places them as volunteers within other charities throughout Britain. Their experience is as varied as the work they do for the charities. For example, apart from the usual business disciplines of management, finance, personnel and marketing, REACH volunteers come from such fields as the civil service, education, the armed forces, health, engineering and the law.

Some REACH volunteers have used their experience to become very effective raisers of the funds themselves. However, most feel this is an area where they do not want to become directly involved, so there is usually a wait of many months for a volunteer to fill any fund-raising job.

REACH's job-finding service is free to both volunteer and voluntary organisation (provided it is a Registered Charity).

For details, phone REACH on 071-928 0452.'

Keith Galpin, REACH Development Manager

JOB DESCRIPTIONS

To give you a starting point, draw up a list of essential tasks then group them under appropriate headings. Basically you need a chairperson or leader, a secretary and a treasurer. Then you might want people to undertake specific jobs like publicity, sponsorship research, events organiser and so on.

Leadership

The right kind of leadership can make or break your cause. Your ideal leader would:

● be totally convinced of your cause's worth and your group's ability to succeed

- have immense personal charisma
- have a strong, confident but not overbearing manner
- have wide-ranging and influential social and business contacts
- be an instinctive and super-efficient coordinator
- know how to delegate wisely
- be an inspiring motivator, with a natural gift for making every individual feel valued
- be someone you can trust not to use your cause to advance his or her personal ambition.

If your group includes someone like that, get that person into the chair as fast as you can. Such paragons are priceless.

Chances are, though, that you'll have to settle for a human being. But try to select a leader whose attitude is both practical and imaginative, who is sincerely dedicated to your cause and who is, above all, positive. A leader who is weak, half-hearted or indecisive, or, conversely, overbearing or intolerant will be a liability rather than an asset. A strong leader brings out the best in everyone.

The secretary

This job needs someone with a good eye for detail and a keen sense of order, who is capable of setting up a simple filing system and who can produce a neat and efficient business letter. Your group's first contact with potential sponsors, donors, supporters, official bodies and the media will probably be made by letter. Nobody will be impressed by poorly presented correspondence. Your letters should reflect the image you want your whole cause to convey — and you can't make a first impression twice. Remember to keep copies of all correspondence, in case of any disputes or misunderstandings.

The secretary should also take minutes at committee meetings. Some committees like to have the minutes typed up and a copy handed to each member at the next meeting. Others use the simpler system where the secretary writes up the minutes in a **Minutes Book** after each meeting. (A large, hard-covered notebook is ideal for this.) The book constitutes a permanent record of all committee decisions, and should be available for inspection by any member.

At the beginning of each meeting the minutes of the previous meeting should be read out for the committee's approval.

The secretary helps the chairperson draw up an **agenda** for each meeting. This document should be duplicated so that everyone attending can see the order of business.

The treasurer

This can be the hardest post to fill. Many people are reluctant to take on the responsibility of looking after money that isn't their own, and get nervous about presenting their records for inspection. The prospect of professional auditing can make them doubly nervous.

In fact, all that's needed is common sense, attention to detail and a competent grasp of arithmetic. There might be someone in your group with accountancy or banking experience who would like the job, but it isn't always best to settle for the obvious. There's more to being a good fund-raising treasurer than keeping the accounts. A housewife, for instance, might make a first-class treasurer. Who better to assess the overall financial position? She budgets the family income, keeps track of commitments and liabilities, weighs up spending power and much else. Consider, too, that a housewife, a shopkeeper or a self-employed business person might have a sharper eye for a bargain and a greater awareness of the commercial aspects of fund-raising. Common sense and astuteness could be more valuable than a narrow discipline.

Two facing pages from a cash book.

The accepted book-keeping practice is to record expenditure on the left-hand (debit) side, and income on the right-hand (credit) side.

1992			1992		
April	£	p	April	£	p
2 1 ream copier paper (Brown's Office Supplies)	2	25	3 Coffee morning (Mrs White)	63	15
5 Crown Hotel Function Room rent (6/3)	35	00	Street collection (29/3)	418	73
Plumbing repairs (Washaway Plumbing)	41	35	10 Nearly New Clothing sale (Mrs Blue)	54	50
15 Book: Finding Sponsors for Community Projects	7	95	17 Cash donation (Sir John Green)	50	00

Figure 1. Example of simple book-keeping.

The treasurer is also responsible for opening a banking account on behalf of the organisation. Shop around the high street banks and building societies to find out what they can offer — many will waive bank charges for charity accounts. You can get information about which building society accounts are best for charity banking from Money Guides in Bury St Edmunds. Money Guides publish a charities edition of their regular newsletter *Building Society Choice*, a constantly updated guide to the best deals currently offered by building societies to charities. Money Guides will send you details and prices of their current guides on request (at the time of writing, *Building Society Choice* costs £12 per annum for 12 monthly issues).

Before you finalise your choice, however, you really should take independent advice from a practising accountant, who will also be able to advise you on the possible pitfalls of putting funds into an interest-accruing account.

QUORUM

You need to decide what number of committee members will constitute a quorum — that is, the minimum number of people who must be present to enable decisions to be taken. The quorum number will depend on the size of your committee, but generally it should consist of at least five members. You should record, too, whether or not the chairperson will have a casting vote in the event of a tied vote.

THE NAME "WINE, WOMEN AND SONG" IS PROBABLY NOT THE BEST NAME FOR A CHARITY!

AN ADDRESS

Your organisation needs an address. If you are operating from independent premises there's no problem, or you might be able to rent space from an existing organisation. If, however, you are working from a member's home, either that member or another would have to be willing to have their address on your letterheads and publicity material. It's best to get settled into a separate headquarters, however small, as soon as possible.

CHECKLIST FOR SETTING UP

Tick when you have: Yes

1. Identified your cause and produced a statement
    defining it.   _____

2. Drafted your constitution.   _____

3. Drafted your ethical guidelines (if applicable).   _____

4. Elected/appointed a leader.   _____

5. Elected/appointed a secretary.   _____

6. elected/appointed a treasurer.   _____

7. Elected/appointed other officers as appropriate.   _____

8. Decided on a quorum.   _____

9. Fixed an address.   _____

2
Charitable Status

SHOULD WE APPLY FOR REGISTRATION?

There are many advantages in becoming a registered charity, and for most organisations these advantages far outweigh the restrictions which registration imposes.

While you're looking at the pros and cons it's a good idea to investigate the charities already active in your area. You might be able to achieve your objectives by working in association with an existing charity. You want to be sure, too, that your aims and objectives will neither overlap nor conflict with a fund-raising appeal that is already up and running.

Short-term appeals
If your cause is to be a one-off appeal which you can realistically expect to complete in a fairly short time, say a few months, it might not be worth applying for registration. It might not come through until it's too late. For some fund-raising purposes, too, you might be able to operate under another charity's umbrella. For example, if you want to provide a piece of equipment for a local hospital, you could be covered by one of the hospital's existing charitable funds. The authority administering the 'umbrella' fund might allow you (or possibly require you) to deposit the money you raise in an account within its own banking arrangements.

Will our objectives qualify as 'charitable'?
The four principal classifications of 'charitable purposes' accepted at law are:

- the relief of poverty
- the advancement of education
- the advancement of learning
- other purposes beneficial to the community in a way that is recognised as charitable.

Fund-raising, you should note, is not a charitable purpose in itself — it must be carried out in support of specified charitable objectives.

The wording of the Objects clause in your constitution must show clearly and unambiguously that your objects comply with these definitions. Try to word the clause in terms specific enough to remove any doubt about your charitable intentions, but broad enough to allow some flexibility. Do take legal advice about this clause, in particular if you decide to apply for registration; once your constitution has been accepted by the Charity Commissioners you can't change your objects without their consent, and that might not be easy to get. The Commissioners will probably also require a description of the activities by which you intend to pursue your objects. They'll scrutinise these to see if the means seem appropriate to the ends, and to ensure that none of your proposed activities fall outside the definition of 'charitable' or appear inappropriate to your capabilities.

Don't make the mistake of declaring an over-ambitious programme that might be beyond your resources and skills. Keep your credibility intact.

Charity Commission leaflet CC21 explains these points in detail, and there are useful guidelines in the Directory of Social Change leaflet *Setting Up*.

What restrictions are imposed by charitable status?

These might not affect your cause, but you should take them into account when you're deciding about applying for registration:

1. A charity cannot undertake certain political and campaigning activities. Take legal advice if this might affect your cause.

2. A charity cannot undertake commercial activity, although it might be possible to set up a separate trading company. Again, take legal advice.

3. A charity must submit accounts to the Charity Commission when requested.

4. There must be no personal benefit to anyone involved in running a charity.

5. Appeals from unregistered groups cannot be considered for funding by grant-making trusts and other bodies which are charitable foundations and bound by the terms of their constitutions.

The advantages

Being a registered charity will undoubtedly make your fund-raising easier and quicker because:

1. Charitable status confers credibility, reassuring donors, supporters and the general public that your cause is genuine and accountable.

2. Generous tax benefits are available for both charities and donors (see below).

3. You'll be eligible for statutory and discretionary rate reliefs.

4. You'll be eligible to apply for grants from a range of sources.

5. Industrial and commercial companies are far more likely to respond to appeals, because they can reap positive benefits by supporting charities.

6. Charities are often able to rent halls, theatres, grounds and other amenities at reduced rates.

7. Many newspapers give charities reduced advertising rates.

8. You should be able to open accounts with wholesale suppliers and cash-and-carry warehouses.

9. It's much easier to get local authority permission to hold public events.

10. You'll be eligible for help from commerce in the form of seconded staff.

11. You'll be eligible to apply for help from REACH volunteers.

TAX ADVANTAGES FOR REGISTERED CHARITIES

Reliefs

Provided the money is used exclusively for charitable purposes, no tax is payable on income, for example rents from land and property, interest and dividends on investments, covenanted donations, grants from other charities and so on.

A charity can also recover tax already deducted from its exempt income by applying to the **Inland Revenue Claims Branch, Charity Division**, who will advise on all tax matters relevant to your cause. Inland Revenue leaflet IR75 explains the areas of exemption and also the circumstances in which exemptions might be restricted.

Be informed
Knowledge of the current tax situation will be an advantage when you come to appeal for donations from individuals and companies. Don't assume that the prospective donor will know about possible benefits. Potential tax savings could be a persuasive argument in your favour — most people are delighted to find legal ways of keeping hard-earned money out of the hands of the Inland Revenue.

Tax reliefs to encourage charitable giving
'The current tax regime in the UK is biased towards encouraging charitable giving,' says Anthony Sober of Lubbock Fine Chartered Accountants, London. 'Individuals are able to obtain tax relief when making donations in the appropriate manner, and charities are able to recover tax that has been deducted from payments made to them.' (Lubbock Fine are experienced in the preparation of tax repayment claims for submission to the Inland Revenue to obtain refunds, and will prepare annual accounts for the charity and arrange for these to be submitted to the Inland Revenue and the Registrar of Charities.)

You can read up on current tax benefits and responsibilities in the relevant Inland Revenue leaflets, which are free from your local tax office. Your group might be able to handle these matters independently — perhaps you're lucky enough to have a chartered accountant among your supporters — but if you're in any doubt about this, do seek professional guidance. There's too much at stake to risk losing donations through lack of knowledge. Ask for the following leaflets:

● IR64: *Giving to Charity: How Businesses Can Get Tax Relief* explains how businesses can claim tax relief through deeds of covenant, secondment of employees, sponsorship payments and donations.

● IR65: *Giving to Charity: How Individuals Can Get Relief* explains the **Payroll Giving Schemes** which enable employees to give to charity directly from their pay and to get tax relief on the payments.

● IR74: *Deeds of Covenant: Getting It Right for Tax* explains that a deed of covenant is a simple way of legally transferring income from one person to another. A deed of covenant covering payments by an individual to a charity must continue for at least four years, while a deed of covenant to a non-charity must continue for at least seven years. Deeds of covenant are governed by strict rules, and it's essential that they be drawn up correctly. Mistakes, however unintentional, can incur penalties.

- IR46: *Income Tax and Corporation Tax* explains these taxes as they might affect clubs, societies and associations.

- IR113: *Gift Aid : A Guide for Donors and Charities* explains the new tax relief introduced in 1990. At the time of writing this relief is relevant to single payments in excess of £600 made to charity by individuals or by companies. The rules for individuals and companies are slightly different, and are fully explained in the leaflet.

Anthony Sober gives an example to illustrate how the relief is applied to a gift from an individual, using current (March 1992) tax rates of 25% basic rate and 40% higher rate:

Gift to charity	£1,500
Tax deemed to have been deducted	£ 500
Gross amount of gift	£2,000
Higher rate relief to taxpayer	£ 300

Thus 'the taxpayer gives the charity £1,500, the charity recovers a further £500 from the tax authorities, and the higher rate taxpayer reduces his higher rate tax bill by £300. The cost to the taxpayer has been a net amount of £1,200, which is the net amount he would have been left with out of an income of £2,000 had he paid tax of 40% on it. Meanwhile the charity has received £2,000.'

While the higher rate tax relief is only obtained by taxpayers liable to pay the higher rates, the same basic principles apply to donations made by any taxpayer of more than £600 by **Gift Aid**, and to donations of any amount, however small, made by **covenant**.

Where payments are made by Gift Aid or covenant, the donor must complete a certificate of deduction of tax, which he or she then gives to

DEED OF COVENANT

Dated:

I . . . .

of . . . .

. . . .

hereby covenant with . . . . (name of the charity

as registered)
. . . .

(hereinafter called the charity) that for a period

of four years from the . . . . day of

. . . . 19 . . . . or during my life

(whichever period be the shorter) I will pay

annually/quarterly/monthly to the charity out of

my taxable income . . . .
(sum in words)

. . . .

signed sealed and delivered by the covenantor

. . . .

In the presence of . . . .

. . . .

Figure 2. Example of a form for a deed of covenant. Note: 1. Covenant payments must be dated to start on or after the date of signing the deed. 2. All deletions should be initialled.

the charity to enable the charity to recover the tax. Certificates are available from the Inland Revenue Claims Branch. Reproductions are printed in leaflet IR113.

Note: Payments by covenant or Gift Aid should only be made out of taxed income. If a donor has no taxed income in the year in question he or she should not make such payments because they will still have to pay the tax over to the authorities so that the charity can recover it.

Legacies

These do not affect income tax in any way. What they do reduce is **Inheritance Tax**. Anyone considering naming a charity in their will should take advice about how such a commitment would affect the tax liabilities on their estate. Inland Revenue leaflet IHT3 *An Introduction to Inheritance Tax* gives the basic information. For full details, ask your tax office for a copy of the 95-page publication IHT1 *Inheritance Tax.*

REGISTRATION

There is no automatic right to registration. The Charity Commissioners consider every application on its merits, and the process can take from two or three months to over a year.

Before you apply, decide which is the most appropriate structure for your organisation. The usual structures are **unincorporated associations, trusts** and **companies**. A solicitor experienced in charity work will advise you on your choice of:

1. An unincorporated association, which is an association, society or club run by a committee elected by its members (officers are personally liable for the association's affairs).

2. A trust, in which a group of people known as trustees ensure that the organisation's funds are properly managed and spent only on the organisation's stated objects (trustees are personally liable for the trust's affairs).

3. A company limited by guarantee: such a company has no shareholders and can't distribute profits to members. The company's directors are responsible for ensuring that its funds are used for its stated purposes, but they have no liability should the company be sued or get into debt (other than by fraudulent intent).

There are different governing documents for each of the above struc-
tures. For more detailed information see Charity Commission leaflet
CC21 *Starting a Charity*, and Directory of Social Change Fund-Raising
Notes leaflet, *Setting Up*. You can also contact the Charity Commission
and/or the National Council for Voluntary Organisations (see Sources of
Advice and Information below).

When you've decided on your structure and drafted your constitution, send
for the questionnaire which the Charity Commissioners produce for new
applicants. They will ask you to send two copies of your draft constitution
with the completed questionnaire, together with any other relevant documents you might have available. Your case will then be assessed, and you
could be asked for further clarification and/or information. The Commissioners might then consult the Inland Revenue before asking you to
formalise your constitution. The Inland Revenue has the power to object
to registration, even if the Charity Commissioners have decided in your
favour, so it's important to sort out any possible problems in advance.

If the Commissioners are satisfied that all is well, they'll write inviting
you to make a formal application, and will send you an official form.

Outside England and Wales
The Charity Commission only deals with organisations active in England
and Wales. There is no formal registration procedure in Scotland or
Northern Ireland. Scottish groups should contact the **Scottish Council for
Voluntary Organisations**, and groups in Northern Ireland should deal
directly with the **Inland Revenue Charity Division Claims Branch** in
Bootle.

Costs
If you can handle your registration yourselves then the costs won't amount
to more than expenses and any charges imposed for setting up your organisation in your chosen form. If you need to employ a solicitor your costs could
run into hundreds of pounds, so choose your legal adviser very carefully.

Registration number
When your registration is approved and complete, you'll be given a
Charity Registration Number. You should display this in all your
correspondence, publicity material and so on.

FURTHER READING

Charitable Status: A Practical Handbook, Andrew Phillips. A step-by-step guide to registering a new charity. Covers constitutional choices and pitfalls, trustees' duties and liabilities, investment powers, ethics and more.

A Guide to Gift Aid, Michael Norton. Explains the details of the scheme and how it can be used in practice, with examples of letters to donors. It also looks at the liberalising changes being made to taxation with regard to charities.

Charity Accounting and Taxation, R.G. Vincent. Comprehensive coverage of tax matters, with advice on tax planning, giving examples from published charity accounts. (Expensive, but should be available in reference libraries.)

Socially Responsible Investment, Sue Ward. Examines the ethical and social implications of investments, with examples, case studies, and sources of information and advice.

Tolley's Charities Manual, subtitled 'The Taxation, Accounts and Audit of Charities'. Deals with setting up a charity, its fund-raising activities, the various forms its accounts may take, the audit of its accounts and the taxation of its income including Value Added Tax. Produced in loose-leaf format, the manual includes 28 appendices containing checklists, regulations, useful addresses, information concerning covenants, model deeds of covenant and other useful information, with many examples. This is an expensive publication at around £50, but you should find it in your public reference library.

SOURCES OF ADVICE AND INFORMATION

The Charity Commission for England and Wales

This is the primary source of advice on all aspects of charitable registration and activity. The Commission has a wide range of powers, and encourages charities and would-be charities to approach them for advice on any matter of concern — there's no charge for this. You'll find a list of the Commission's leaflets in the appendices.

Action Match

See the section on Social Sponsorship, Chapter 5.

Action Resource Centre

A national voluntary organisation with a network of area offices. Its activities include transferring business skills and resources to community organisations, with priority given to those dealing with inner city problems; promoting and arranging secondment; providing advice and management training to community groups; running a community accountancy service.

ACRE (Action with Communities in Rural England)

This is a charity 'taking action on jobs, housing, transport, shops and other services in rural areas'. ACRE is the national association of England's 38 Rural Community Councils (RCCs) and works at local and national levels to provide information, advice, training and action 'to improve the quality of life of all those living and working in our countryside'.

RCCs are county-level charities, in touch with parish councils, village halls, schools, youth groups, Women's Institutes and local voluntary organisations. Among their various services, they advise on fund-raising, legal obligations, safety matters and so on. ACRE and RCCs produce various publications including, for example, *Rural Advice and Information: Setting Up a Local Service*; a *Directory of National Charitable Guilds and Trusts,* which identifies over 250 of the smaller guilds, trusts and charitable companies operating from London with a national remit; *Negotiating Grants: Issues for Local Authorities and Voluntary Groups*; and a *Parish Appraisal*s pack, with information and ideas for parish councils and voluntary groups particularly concerned with environmental aspects of parish or village appraisals.

ACRE also publishes *Rural Viewpoint*, a news magazine covering ACRE's interests.

ACRE will send you a list of current publications plus information about the organisation — what it can do for you, and what you can do for ACRE — on request.

The Charities Aid Foundation (CAF)

Established in 1924, the Charities Aid Foundation exists to help and coordinate the raising and distribution of funds to other charities. Its services include handling, for donors, covenanted accounts, Give As You Earn, and various trust and legacy schemes. For charities they run a number of successful investment schemes and the Covenant Management Centre. CAF has extensive information and research departments from which both donors and charities can benefit.

CAF publications include *The Directory of Grant-Making Trusts,* which gives details of the location, policies and resources of over 2,500 grant-making bodies — a valuable reference source for fund-seekers. Published every two years, this 1,000-page treasury of information costs about £50, but should be available in reference libraries.

CAF also produces a Charity Events Calendar, a reference work giving the latest information supplied by charities about their fund-raising and publicity events. Each issue of the calendar covers a 12-month period with up-dates every three months, and is designed to help charities plan their activities and events so that they don't clash with others. CAF describes the calendar as 'an essential reference for:

- companies looking for local charitable events to support
- PR companies looking for charitable events with which their clients wish to be associated
- local newspapers who wish to cover local charity events
- libraries and information services needing to know what's happening where and when
- charities (as well as supporting volunteers and organisations) planning new events.'

A single copy of the calendar costs £15, with reduced rates for longer-term subscriptions.

CAF publications include *Sources of Charity Finance*, edited by Norman Lee, a collection of research papers on sources of charity finance.

CAF also publishes a monthly magazine, *Charity*, 'a forum for new ideas in giving and fund-raising, new trends in administration, legislation and evaluation'. A well produced 40-page A4 magazine, *Charity* carries news, views, profiles, reports, book reviews, articles on management, development, finance, legislation, fund-raising, and charity-related advertising. The yearly subscription is £30, and you can obtain a single copy for £1.75 plus postage. *Charity* could be very useful to your cause, both as a source of information and as a platform for your own views.

The Directory of Social Change

This is an educational charity which undertakes research and provides information, advice and training to the voluntary sector. The Directory of Social Change publishes a range of guides and handbooks, and will send their publications list and training course programme on request. Courses particularly relevant to your cause might be 'Basic Fund-Raising', 'Developing a Sponsorship Proposal' and 'Developing a Fund-Raising Strategy'.

Your early reading might usefully include the Directory's set of *Fund-Raising Notes*, comprising 12 A4 leaflets (the number of pages varies) giving much useful information along with many contact addresses. You'll find a list of the leaflets in the appendices. It's worth having the complete set (cheaper, too), although a few of the leaflets need a bit of up-dating with regard to addresses. The advice they offer doesn't date, though.

CharityFair 1992 is a new project set up by the Directory. If the venture is successful, which is very likely given the increasingly high profile and competitive nature of the voluntary sector, no doubt it will become a regular event. Ask for information when you send for the publications list.

InterChange Advisory Services

Operating within the InterChange Trust, InterChange Advisory Services can advise on fund-raising, financial management, registration, constitutions, etc. They run Management Training Courses which include fund-raising, management, planning and decision-making. Details of all their services are available on request.

London Voluntary Service Council (LVSC)

Funded by the London Boroughs Grants Committee, LVSC runs training courses, meetings and conferences on community and voluntary work. LVSC publishes a newsletter for London's voluntary groups, *Voluntary Voice*, published ten times a year. A subscription to the newsletter also covers their *Training Directory*, published three times a year.

LVSC Publications List, available on request, includes two books which would be particularly useful to any group in the process of setting up: *Voluntary But Not Amateur* (third edition) is 'a guide to the law for voluntary organisations and community groups' and is packed with advice and contact addresses, including fund-raising sources.

Just About Managing? is 'a guide to effective management for voluntary organisations and community groups' covering, among other topics, management committees and meetings, team-work and decision-making, managing training, time and money, and managing conflict and stress. You'll probably find both these books available for reference at CVS centres (see below) and you can buy them direct from LVSC.

National Association of Councils for Voluntary Service (NACVS)

NACVS is an association of more than 200 Councils for Voluntary Service (CVS) spread throughout the country. Its purpose is to support and develop local voluntary action.

Having previously operated as part of the National Council for Voluntary Organisations (NCVO), in April 1991 NACVS became a fully independent national organisation with its offices in Sheffield. NACVS will continue to be a member of NCVO, cooperating on national voluntary sector initiatives and retaining access to NCVO resources and services (see below).

NACVS is supported by the Voluntary Services Unit at the Home Office, but like all such organisations there is always a need for funding and an appeal has been launched to charitable trusts and the private sector for funds to develop its work with local CVS.

CVS members represent voluntary bodies, local authorities and statutory bodies working in partnership, and each branch is largely funded by local sources. CVS branches are run autonomously to meet the perceived needs of the local community, and functions vary from area to area, but the whole organisation works on the simple principle that 'when resources are scarce and expensive, it makes sense to pool the resources we have'.

Contact NACVS headquarters for the address of your nearest CVS, which you can approach for advice and guidance on all aspects of your cause. They'll tell you about other amenities and services available at that particular CVS. (For example, the CVS Centre at St Thomas's, Ardwick Green, Manchester, has a comprehensive reference library of publications produced by and for people involved in all kinds of community and voluntary work, and also runs a widely used printing service.)

NACVS will also send you a catalogue of 175 publications costing from nothing at all up to around £5.

National Council for Voluntary Organisations (NCVO)

NCVO is a well informed source of advice and information to help existing or potential organisations. They'll advise on charity law, registration procedures, fund-raising — everything concerned with voluntary work. A publications stocklist is available on request, covering all current NCVO/Bedford Square Press publications. (Bedford Square Press is NCVO's publishing imprint.)

There are several departments dealing with the various aspects of voluntary work, all based at the same address.

National Federation of Community Organisations (NFCO)

NFCO is a nationwide federation of community organisations offering advice, information and practical help to local groups. They can also provide a model constitution approved by the Charity Commission.

Voluntary Services Unit, The Home Office

See under Government Grants, Chapter 6.

CHECKLIST FOR CHARITABLE STATUS

Tick when you have: Yes

1. Sent for relevant Charity Commission leaflets.   ____

2. Read *Charitable Status* by Andrew Phillips.   ____

3. Sent for the Directory of Social Change
   Fund-raising Notes.   ____

4. Contacted appropriate sources for further advice if
   necessary (for example, the Charity Commissioners,
   National Council for Voluntary Organisations, Inland
   Revenue Claims Branch, Charity Division)   ____

5. Fully discussed the pros and cons of registering as a
   charity, if applicable.   ____

6. Made a decision on whether or not to apply.   ____

7. If 'yes', set an application in motion.   ____

INDEPENDENT CONSULTANTS

You might consider investing some of your resources in the services of
an independent consultant. Such a consultant could save you a great deal
of time and energy — and money, too — by showing you how to use your
present and future resources in the most suitable, efficient and cost-effective ways when you're planning your fund-raising.

Independent consultant Barbara Keeley-Huggett works with both large
and small organisations. Here she describes how the independent consultant fits into the overall scheme of things.

'Newcomers to community organisations and the voluntary sector may
be surprised at the range and depth of support available to them. The main
difficulty is just finding out about and getting in touch with the people
who can help.

'The voluntary sector support network can be described in terms of the
various organisations, and what they do:

- Umbrella or intermediary organisations such as the National Council for Voluntary Organisations or the local Council for Voluntary Service.

- Specialist intermediary organisations such as Action Resource Centre or Action Match.

- Organisations such as the Directory of Social Change which publish guides and run training programmes.

'Yet this picture is not complete without knowing that alongside these organisations there is also a network of independent consultants. These consultants are sometimes working alone, or sometimes in association with other independents. For example, in the last 12 months I have run a workshop at an NCVO conference, completed a survey for Action Match, worked with Action Resource Centre on promoting secondment and have been the tutor on courses for Directory of Social Change. I have also helped smaller organisations to design a survey, plan their fund-raising strategy, and have trained staff to become confident speakers.

'I switched to being an independent consultant and trainer after a successful 17 year career with IBM. This career gave me experience of marketing, training and managing people. I decided to use this knowledge working in the ''socially useful'' sector of the economy. Working from a base at home (like many independents) means that overheads can be kept down. For organisations like Action Resource Centre and the Directory of Social Change, it makes sense to use consultants on a freelance basis when they have a piece of work to be done, or training to be run.

'Smaller organisations can be put in touch with independent consultants through the intermediary organisations. The Management Unit at NCVO gives advice on selecting consultants, and the other organisations help to put people in touch with consultants they know.

'Independents carry all their own costs, and so the fees for the work they do have to reflect this. If I were working for a commercial management consultancy my time would be charged out at a rate from £400 to £800 per day or more. As an independent in the voluntary sector, my fees in 1991 have been £200 per day, plus travel costs.'

Barbara Keeley-Huggett

3
Organising Your Appeal

However local the scope of your project and your appeal, you can learn a lot from the strategies used by major national appeals, most of which benefit from the expertise of professional fund-raisers. In an interview published in a BBC Education booklet titled *The Giving Business*, Marion Allford, Director of the Wishing Well Appeal, outlined the three vital phases of a successful appeal. These are:

- Phase 1: research and planning
- Phase 2: the private appeal
- Phase 3: the public appeal.

The Wishing Well Appeal, which raised funds for substantial rebuilding at the Hospital for Sick Children, Great Ormond Street, London, was planned on a five-year timetable: two years for research, planning and recruitment, one year for the private appeal, and a further two years for the public appeal. In the event, the public appeal achieved — and passed — its target in only one year, so thorough was the work done during the first two phases. The Wishing Well Appeal raised £54 million a year ahead of its estimated completion date.

Your own target won't be anywhere near that gigantic figure, of course, or your timetable so long-term, but this tried and proven method is a good model to follow when you're thinking through your own strategies.

PHASE 1: RESEARCH

1. List everything that might affect your project's feasibility, however remotely. For example, if your plans include buying, renovating, converting or building property, it's essential to contact your local planning department straight away. You'll need **planning permission**, and that takes time however straightforward the application. You need to make sure, too, that no one is likely to come along in a

couple of years and bulldoze your project under a motorway or a bypass.

2. Find out as many facts and figures as possible to substantiate your claim that the community needs your project. If you want to set up, say, a day-care and play centre for under-fives you'll add a lot of clout to your case if you can produce statistics showing, for example

- the total lack, scarcity or expense of existing facilities
- the number of children under five living in the area
- the number of births registered in the area over the past year
- the number of working mothers
- the number of single-parent families

Vague claims of 'an urgent need' are meaningless without hard evidence to back them up.

The Directory of Social Change leaflet *Doing Research* shows you how to use Census data to get the information you need.

3. Obtain estimates of as many of your expected costs as you can. How much will it cost, for example, to rent operational premises, instal a telephone, pay for legal advice, have stationery printed and so on? You might be able to get at least some of these necessities donated, but at this early stage you need to know what costs you could be committed to covering.

4. Make a list of people who might be willing and able to help your cause in any way: influential citizens, key business personnel, councillors, your MP, your MEP (Member of the European Parliament), the editor of your local newspaper, and so on. These are some of the people you'll be contacting in Phase 2.

5. Make a list of companies who might be interested in supporting your project with donations of money, gifts in kind, sponsorship and so on — see under Chapter 5, Help From Industry and Commerce. Find out the names of their key personnel.

6. Make a list of other possible sources of funding that might be receptive to your cause, including individual benefactors, grant-making bodies, national fund-raising events and so on.

7. List all existing local organisations that might be willing to help: Round Table, Ladies' Circles, Lions and Leos, Freemasons, clubs, and the like.

8. Make contact with other local charitable groups, to find out their scope of activity and future fund-raising plans. You don't want to tread on toes by duplicating or clashing with their planned events.

9. Consider the possible value of investing in advice and/or training in fund-raising, either from one of the organisations who run regular courses or from an independent fund-raising consultant. See under 'Sources of advice and information' in Chapter 2.

10. Read, read, read — the more you know the more confident you'll feel and the more convincing and authoritative your approaches to potential donors will be.

Information held on computer

Under the Data Protection Act 1984, anyone holding information on computer about any identifiable living person must have the signed permission of those people to do so, and must register under the Act. (The Act doesn't cover information kept on card index systems or in filing cabinets.) For further information contact the Office of the Data Protection Registrar.

Image

Give some thought to the image you want your appeal to convey to the public. Don't underestimate the importance of giving the right impression. Every letter you send, every piece of publicity material you distribute, makes a silent statement about you and your attitude to your cause and to potential donors. You need to get the pitch just right, to reflect your concerns and to show that you're enthusiastic and efficient but not extravagant.

Study the literature that arrives through all our letter-boxes from various appeals. Do glossy, slick, multi-coloured brochures make you uneasy about how those organisations are spending the money they raise? On the other hand, do you look doubtfully at flimsy, badly produced leaflets and wonder whether their senders are competent to be running an appeal?

Your immediate reactions probably reflect those of most citizens. Make sure your own cause's image doesn't give any wrong impressions.

(It might be a good investment to get professional help with designing and writing your stationery, leaflets and brochures. Perhaps an eye-catching logo, a specific colour, would be effective in identifying your cause to the public. There's a useful directory available that lists freelance writers and artists countrywide, with details of the services they offer. *The Publisher's Freelance Directory* is published annually by Hobson's.)

If your cause has an environmental connection (or just because you want to) you could use recycled materials for at least some of your stationery needs. You'll find advertisements of suppliers in craft and environmental magazines. Lancashire company The Cutting Edge, for example, supplies a range of goods made from recycled materials, such as stationery, card blanks, bookmarks, gift tags, printed labels, carrier bags, display stands and so on. This particular company also offers a service for cutting cloth and card to the customer's specifications. Partner Kevin McCarthy says that the company works on a small profit margin, to keep prices as low as possible. He gives generous discounts for quantity buying, for example white envelopes size 133 x 185mm (about $5^1/_4$ x $7^1/_4$ in) made from 100% recycled paper cost about 6 pence each when bought singly, but purchases of 100 at £4.25 or 1,000 at £29.85 work out at 4.25 pence and 3 pence per envelope respectively. (Prices quoted are approximate, and might vary with changes in VAT or the rate of inflation.) These are rock bottom prices, and Kevin says he'd love to be able to offer further discounts to charities but at the moment it just isn't possible to do so and survive.

Write for details and a price list, or ring Kevin McCarthy.

Professional fund-raisers

You might want to consider hiring a professional fund-raiser to organise your appeal for you. These are people whose business is raising funds for others, and they're usually skilled and experienced in the work, so in some cases it might be advantageous to use them. You should bear the following points in mind:

1. Fees can be charged in either of two ways: by a set fee for time and services, or by payment of a proportion of the money raised. It's important to be clear which method is involved before entering into any agreement. (Most reputable fund-raisers use the 'set fee' system.) You should also establish whether the fee will be paid in a lump sum or spread over periodic payments. These details should be agreed in writing to avoid any possibility of future disputes.

2. Let the public know. When professional fund-raisers are being used,

you should always make it clear to the giving public that part of their donations will be spent on paying fees.

Budgeting

A budget is a programme of expenditure and income. In these early stages your figures are likely to rely largely on educated guesswork, but you should put a budget plan down on paper just the same. Seeing the figures in black and white will focus your mind on financial reality which can sometimes get clouded in rosy optimism.

Expenditure

Item	Cash cost	Means	Who to approach
——————	£ ———	———	——————
——————	£ ———	———	——————
——————	£ ———	———	——————
——————	£ ———	———	——————
——————	£ ———	———	——————

Estimated in-come source	Amount	When expected	Coordinating member
——————	£ ———	———	——————
——————	£ ———	———	——————
——————	£ ———	———	——————
——————	£ ———	———	——————
——————	£ ———	———	——————

You could clarify the picture further by adopting a rating system on the lines of A = highly probable, B = quite likely, C = possible, D = difficult but worth a try.

Figure 3. Budget layout.

You need to estimate in as much detail as you can what your appeal and your project will cost, and how, where and when you can find the means to meet those costs. Your budget isn't chiselled in stone — it's a working instrument and you can revise it as and when necessary.

Make a list of all the expenditure you foresee. Start with the basic essentials like rent and rates, telephone, professional services and so on. Then include equipment like office furniture, a typewriter, transport — whatever is necessary to get your cause set up. Beside each item, note its cost, either actual or estimated (it's better to over-estimate rather than under-estimate). In another column note every reasonable means by which you might be able to get that item — as a gift-in-kind, by sponsorship, bought with a cash donation, on loan . . . Use imagination and ingenuity to keep cash expenditure as low as possible.

You also need to estimate the income you can reasonably hope for.

Setting all this down should enable you to assess the overall financial picture, and should help you identify strengths and weaknesses in your strategy.

If your cause involves an on-going project, it's a good idea to draw up an additional budget (see Figure 3), in as much detail as you can, for future running costs. The more you can demonstrate a responsible approach to finance, the stronger will be your credibility.

CHECKLIST FOR RESEARCH

Tick when you have: Yes   Member/officer
                                                              responsible

1. Checked out planning permission/
    other possible obstacles. Specify: ☐   _____

2. Compiled relevant statistics.   ☐   _____

3. Estimated costs.   ☐   _____

4. Identified potential individual supporters.   ☐   _____

5. Identified potential company supporters. ☐   _____

6. Listed other possible funding sources.   ☐   _____

7. Identified other local charities currently
    seeking funding.   ☐   _____

8. Evaluated cost and desirability of paying for advice/training. ☐ _____

9. Obtained relevant reading matter. ☐ _____

10. Outlined your budget. ☐ _____

PHASE 1: PLANNING

Plan Phases 2 and 3 in as much detail as you possibly can. Coordination is vital, so make sure everybody involved knows:

- what you plan to do
- when you plan to do it
- how you plan to do it
- who will take overall responsibility for each activity.

It's essential to avoid working at cross purposes or overlapping your approaches to individuals and businesses. Misunderstandings could lead to your organisation being regarded as inefficient and therefore not to be trusted to make the best use of donations.

Step-by-step

1. Work out realistic timetables, taking into account the number of people available and the amount of time they can spend on the work.

Generally speaking, Phases 1 and 2 will need at least two or three months, to allow for detailed preparation for Phase 3.

The duration of Phase 3 itself will depend on how ambitious your target is. Do aim, though, to achieve your goal by a specified date. A deadline focuses everyone's attention on the need to get on with things, and offers a far greater challenge than any open-ended time-scale.

2. Make a list of the fund-raising activities and events your group sees as the most potentially effective, suitable and within your capabilities and budget. Be specially careful about the last two points. It's only too easy to let over-enthusiasm dazzle you into committing yourself to a big, glamorous event that's beyond your ability to run efficiently, or your means to meet its expenses. Throw out anything that might leave you out of pocket.

Allocate responsibility for each agreed event to someone capable of organising it. Each organiser should know exactly what is expected of them, and everyone else should know, too, so there's no risk of misunderstandings or interference. These can so easily lead to friction.

3. Make a list of possible publicity outlets for Phase 3, and plan the most appropriate and effective means by which to get that publicity. Every event you plan will have different needs — identify them early, so you don't find on the eve of the event that you've forgotten to get the posters printed, or you've left it too late to sell advertising space in the programmes you planned to sell in advance.

CHECKLIST FOR PLANNING

Tick when you have: Yes

1. Worked out a manageable timetable for   _____

    Phase 2: the private appeal   _____

    Phase 3: the public appeal.   _____

2. Set a deadline for achieving your target.   _____

3. Listed proposed fund-raising activities and events. _____

4. Allocated responsibility for such activities and events. _____

5. Listed publicity outlets and means of using them.   _____

A written report
The last stage of Phase 1 is the production of a summary of the decisions you've taken and the preparatory work you've already done. The main purpose of this summary is to show potential donors and supporters — as well as existing ones — that you've thought the whole project through, are tackling it in an efficient and pragmatic way, and that any help they give you will be used in the most cost-effective way possible. In other words, that you're credible and trustworthy. Confidence is the name of the game at this stage.

The summary should contain such information as

● an outline of your project and its aims and objectives

- why you believe the community needs your project (backed up with facts and figures from your research)
- who will benefit
- how much the project will cost to set up (backed up with estimates and quotes)
- the estimated running costs (if this applies)
- how you propose to raise the money
- your fund-raising programme and timetable.

If your group includes people with knowledge, skills and experience directly relevant to the project, give this information. It could be a plus point, too, if prominent and respected citizens are already involved. It would certainly do no harm to mention them (with their agreement).

PHASE 2: THE PRIVATE APPEAL

Now you should be ready to approach the potential funding sources you've identified during your research. These could include:

1. Grant-making bodies; see Chapter 3, Looking for Grants.

2. Individuals who might be willing to covenant money to your cause, to give (or pledge) donations — perhaps there's a philanthropic millionaire living in the community — or give practical help such as the use of a large garden, a field or a barn, or the loan of equipment.

3. Companies you've assessed as potentially sympathetic to your cause — see Chapter 5, Help from Industry and Commerce.

Some groups arrange a lunch or evening party for invited guests whom they've identified as potential donors, or who represent possible donor companies. If you do something like this, take care not to overdo the hospitality. Keep it to an appropriate level — you won't do your cause any good by appearing to throw money around. If you already have premises where your project will be housed, you could invite your guests to make a tour while you explain your plans. Lay on modest refreshments afterwards, to encourage people to stay on and discuss the project with you and with each other.

Perhaps you could mount some kind of visual display showing, for example, proposed plans for the layout, outlines of the various activities your project will offer, pictures of the kind of equipment you'll need. . .

anything that will show potential donors that you're tackling the project sensibly and efficiently. Visual impressions will stick in people's minds, and will add impact to the literature you provide and any explanatory talk you might give. Have copies of your prepared report available.

Alternatively — and in some cases this might be more appropriate and effective — make appointments to see the key personnel you've already identified at their places of business. Take along your prepared literature, plans and so on, and try to anticipate the kind of questions you're likely to be asked. Confidence and an unshakeable faith in the worth of your cause are your greatest assets.

With either of the above approaches, you might be offered immediate help in the form of cash or equipment, or you might be given pledges of help to be delivered at some later stage. You might, in fact almost certainly you will, get some refusals. Accept these decisions gracefully, and thank those concerned for giving you their time. Don't shut any doors — there might be a change of mind (or a change of personnel) at some later date.

This is also the time to take action on some of your other decisions, such as:

● applying for the necessary licences if your plans for Phase 3 include a street collection and/or a large-scale prize draw — it can sometimes take quite a while to get such permissions
● booking suitable venues for planned events — many popular venues get booked up months, even years, ahead
● booking any groups or bands you'll need for functions — see under 'Live music' in Chapter 7
● booking speakers and celebrities.

Make an appointment to visit your local newspaper office, to get to know the editor and other key staff. Discuss your project and your fund-raising plans. Bringing the local press into the picture this early allows time for them to think about how they might help you when you launch Phase 3, and for you to sound them out about future support. A friendly, trusting relationship here will be invaluable.

PHASE 3: THE PUBLIC APPEAL

You've done your homework, made your plans, established your contacts and taken action to organise as many fund-raising events as you think you can cope with. You're ready to 'go public'.

Peter Pan Play Project

Pond Lane, Shakybridge

NEWS FOR RELEASE

BARNABY BIGBOOKS IS COMING TO TOWN!

World-famous children's author BARNABY BIGBOOKS will make a very special visit to Pond Lane next Saturday morning.

Barnaby is touring the country giving readings from his latest blockbusting bestseller GHOSTIES AND GHOULIES. He'll be taking time off to open our new play centre for the under-fives at St Michael's Hall, Pond Lane at 10.30am.

Barnaby heard about the PETER PAN PLAY PROJECT from his aunt Mrs Ivy Pink, whose grandson Bobby Bright brought his Mum, Betty, and his Grandma Ivy for a behind-the-scenes peep at the play centre last week.

Barnaby is very keen to meet as many children as he can, so come along and say Hello!

See you there — at the PETER PAN PLAY PROJECT, St Michael's Hall, Pond Lane, Shakybridge at 10.30 on Saturday 10th of April.

Figure 4. Example of a press release

Make your launch a good one: get the impetus going with as much publicity as possible and at least one high-profile event to catch the public's interest, preferably with a celebrity or a well known local figure in attendance.

Publicity

The good relationship you've taken care to establish with the local press will prove its worth now. A fanfare announcement of the launch of your appeal, and a prominent editorial feature about your project, the people working for it, and its value to the community should get you off to that vital flying start.

The feature should declare your fund-raising target and should include an outline of your planned programme of events, with dates and venues, encouraging anyone who would like to help your cause in any way to contact your group.

If there's a human interest story connected with your enterprise (perhaps it was a specific human problem that triggered the whole thing off) this could make a strong emotional impact on the public. Make sure, though, that you have the specific permission of the person or persons involved before you make public any details like their names, photographs, circumstances and so on. Get their permission *in writing*, for your own protection. People sometimes change their minds, or even forget what they've agreed to, so you need evidence of their consent in case of future disputes.

Individuals and companies who have already made or pledged donations might appreciate a public acknowledgement, which could also act as an encouragement to other potential supporters. Check with them first, though. Some people prefer not to have this kind of gesture brought to public notice. You must respect their wishes, whatever their reasons.

Ongoing support

As your appeal progresses keep the editor in the picture about your activities and their success, so that he can keep your appeal in the public eye. Make the paper's job as easy as you can by sending prepared press releases and reports on your events, with black-and-white photographs for visual interest.

Remember to invite the editor and appropriate members of his staff to important functions. It's wise, however, to specify the number of people you're extending the invitation to — it's not unknown for an open invitation to be interpreted as applying to the entire staff.

Local radio

This is a very underused publicity resource. Ring up the managers of your local stations and tell them what you're doing, what kind of story you can offer, and what you need publicity for — your cause as a whole and/or a specific event.

Have all the facts in front of you, so you can give any information asked for without wasting time. Offer to send your literature, press cuttings and so on.

You might be offered air time to put your cause before the public yourself. You need someone who can enunciate clearly and talk fluently, to make the most of such a chance.

You can find the addresses and telephone numbers of BBC and independent local radio stations in the *Writers' & Artists' Yearbook*. A current copy should be available at your local library.

The talk circuit

You can get very useful publicity — and often support, too — by giving talks on your project to schools and colleges, local clubs and societies. Comb your local press for reports on club activities — you'll find that most papers have a column for these — and note the organiser's name. There's often a phone number given for membership enquiries.

Publicity material

Your printed publicity material is your other main contact with the public. It should project the desired image as well as the right information. Every brochure, every leaflet, every poster, every programme should be clear, concise, correct and complete:

- **Clear:** choose easy-to-read type and simple words that are quickly and easily absorbed and understood.

- **Concise:** don't clutter up your message with elaborate prose — cut out all unnecessary words and phrases.

- **Correct:** make sure all the information is accurate; double check that events, venues, days, dates, times, directions, celebrities' names, titles and so on are accurate and correctly spelled.

- **Complete:** double check that all essential information is there; that is, everything the recipient of a letter or press release, or the reader of a leaflet or poster, needs and wants to know.

Mega-Brilliant
Posters and leaflets for events designed to attract children should be 'Super-Colossal', 'Fantastic', 'Mammoth', 'Gy-normous'. . . Get the latest 'in' words from youngsters themselves.

Early funding

By now you might be wondering where the money is to come from to fund all these preliminary activities. There are several possibilities. For example, if your plans are quite modest it might be enough to have a whip-round among your group and sympathisers. Or you could set up a membership list and invite people to make a small contribution of a membership fee which would entitle them to, for instance, entry to a Members' Marquee at your summer garden party, reserved seats at fund-raising events, an acknowledgement in events programmes and so on.

You could also ask members of your group to run (and to ask their friends to run) small fund-raising events like coffee mornings, sales parties. These can provide the 'seed-corn' funds that underpin your initial expenses and the necessary outlay for preparing larger events. You'll find some suggestions for such events later in the book. Don't forget to thank everyone who helps raise these early funds — they'll appreciate a personal letter. It's never too early to start building goodwill.

'Friends'

If you want to put your supporters on a slightly more organised and formal footing, set up a 'Friends of. . .' network. This can work very well as it gives people a sense of belonging, almost a 'family' feeling for the cause.

4
Looking for Grants

GRANTS FROM EUROPE

It isn't easy to get money from the **European community**, but organisations which have applied successfully have benefited by substantial amounts, in some cases as much as £1,000,000.

The criteria for eligibility and the procedures for applications and assessment are very complex and, like much other EC business, subject to frequent alteration. Faced with these shifting goalposts, your best course is to seek advice from the **National Council for Voluntary Organisations**, whose experts keep in touch with the situation as it currently applies.

Your Euro-Constituency Member of the European Parliament (MEP) might also be able to help, possibly even lobbying on your behalf. (If you're not sure where to locate your MEP, contact the London Office of the European Parliament.)

Recommended reading
Grants From Europe (6th edition) by Ann Davison and Bill Seary. Subtitled 'How to get money and influence policy', this is a comprehensive guide to the various EC funding programmes, detailing the departments, with contact names in both London and Brussels. It lists key publications relevant to each programme, tells you how and where to apply for grants, and looks at problems you might encounter.

GRANTS FROM CENTRAL GOVERNMENT

While Central Government will not normally fund purely local projects directly, it sometimes helps experimental or innovatory projects that might eventually prove significant nationally. As with many government policies, criteria for eligibility tend to be altered frequently, and it's certainly worth taking advice about possible government funding. These are the main departments, with some examples (not exhaustive) of the type of projects they might consider:

1. **Department of Education and Science**
   - voluntary youth organisations
   - adult education
   - educational services and research

2. **Department of the Environment** (which will send you a free guide to its grants)
   - projects to relieve homelessness
   - the **Urban Programme**, a range of schemes including community centres, arts projects, children's play schemes, projects for old or disabled people, repair of listed buildings and ancient monuments
   - the **Special Grants Programme**, including practical and educational projects for regenerating urban areas, and conservation of the natural or man-made world.

3. **Department of Health**
   - voluntary children's homes
   - assisted community homes
   - day care for under-fives
   - combating drug and alcohol abuse

4. **The Home Office:** the **Voluntary Services Unit** at the Home Office will advise you about eligibility for grants from any government department, and will put you in touch with liaison officers in the appropriate department. These officers will advise on grant availability and current application procedures.
   The Voluntary Services Unit itself has a limited amount of money which it allocates for the support of cost-effective voluntary activity, including:
   - marriage guidance councils (recently renamed 'Relate')
   - rehabilitation of offenders
   - crime prevention
   - victim support
   - refugee projects

Grants guides
The Directory of Social Change publishes a number of grants guides,

including *The Central Government Grants Guide, The Educational Grants Directory, A Guide to Grants for Individuals in Need, The London Grants Guide, Environmental Grants* and *The Arts Funding Guide.*

Quangos
(Quasi-autonomous non-governmental organisations)
These organisations are empowered to allocate government money. If any seem appropriate to your project, it's worth making enquiries:

● Arts Council of Great Britain
● British Film Institute
● Commission for Racial Equality
● Countryside Commission
● Crafts Council
● Equal Opportunities Commission
● Nature Conservancy Council
● Sports Council

For advice and information on all the above, consult the National Council for Voluntary Organisations.

Recommended reading
It could pay your group to invest in a copy of *Government Grants: A Guide for Voluntary Organisations* (6th Edition), compiled by Maggie Jones and published by NCVO (Bedford Square Press). This is a very helpful handbook for all voluntary groups hoping to raise money from official sources. Packed with detailed advice, information, addresses, even contact names, it could be the key to some of the funding you need.

GRANTS FROM LOCAL AUTHORITIES

Local authority funding is becoming tighter, but if you can put up a convincing case and make an effective application, you might get significant funding from this source.

Before you set any application in train, find out whether your project is compatible with your local authority's powers to make grants (some are restricted by policy), and with its priorities, as no authority these days has the resources to fund every project, however sympathetically viewed. In the main, grants are allocated by:

● county authorities
● district or borough councils

- town or parish councils
- local education authorities.

Take time to find out how your target authority makes grant decisions, who are the right people to contact, and how the authority likes applications to be presented. (If you have or can establish personal contacts there, so much the better. Influential representation and lobbying will maximise your chances.)

Your application is also more likely to succeed if you can relate your cause's aims and objectives to needs which the local authority has already identified in the community. Homework in these areas will equip you to make the most effective application.

Recommended reading

Directory of Social Change leaflets *Fund-raising Sources* and *Writing an Application* give advice on this, as does Maggie Jones's book *Government Grants* (see above). NCVO can also advise you.

GRANT-MAKING TRUSTS

Grant-making trusts (often called foundations) are privately set up organisations usually funded by investment income from money endowed by their founders. They exist for the purpose of distributing money to charitable causes.

Most grant-making trusts are only empowered to grant money to registered charities, although some are able to make discretionary exceptions.

There are thousands of such trust funds in the UK, some huge and handling millions of pounds, some quite small and local. You need to identify the trust fund or funds which might be interested in your particular field of activity. The most accessible source of information is the *Directory of Grant-Making Trusts*, published every two years by the Charities Aid Foundation. This is an expensive publication, costing around £50, but you should find it in your reference library or at your local Council for Voluntary Service. The CVS might also keep a register of small local trusts (these won't be listed in the *Directory of Grant-Making Trusts*).

You might also get information about local charities from your local council offices, and about parochial charities from your parish church — many such charities make funds available to local causes.

The Charities Aid Foundation and the National Council for Voluntary Organisations are there to help as well.

Mr John Moneypurse
Borough Treasurer
Shakybridge Borough Council

Dear Mr Moneypurse

We are a group of residents who plan to set up a play centre for children under five years of age living in our community.

We believe there is a great need for such a centre, where children will be able to play and absorb social skills under responsible and qualified supervision in a bright, stimulating, safe environment.

Our centre will also provide a second service: a room where the children's parents can, if they wish, relax and get to know each other over a cup of tea or coffee. This complementary function will do much, we believe, to alleviate the sense of isolation and loneliness that troubles many young parents in our community today and which all too often leads to or aggravates family problems, thus increasing the work-load of local social services.

No service of this kind exists within reasonable travelling distance of Shakybridge, other than two privately run day-care/child-minding services both of which are well beyond the pocket of most young families. There will be no charge for children using our play centre, and refreshments for parents will be charged at cost.

As you know, last year our local Society of Arts, Crafts and Literature bought the redundant church of St Michael in Pond Lane in the Sunnyside district. The society has offered our project the use of the church hall for a minimum lease of ten years.

Over the last three months we have been researching the project's feasibility, particularly with regard to costs. We find that essential repairs to the fabric of the hall plus the installation of up-to-date plumbing and electrical wiring would cost about £12,000. (Please see the enclosed estimates.)

As soon as the basic work is done, we shall be able to take up pledges of paint for redecoration (A & B White & Co), flooring (Neverslip Tiles Ltd), basic furniture (Nutwood Ltd) and play equipment (Mad Hatter Toy Company).

Can you help us please, with a grant to cover all or part of the £12,000 we need to put the building in order?

I enclose a copy of a report on our research findings and our financial plans.

Yours sincerely

Angela Youngheart
Chair, Peter Pan Play Project

Figure 5. Example of a letter of application for a grant from a local authority.

APPLYING FOR A GRANT

Make sure your application covers every relevant aspect. If the body you're approaching produces an application form, read it all the way through before beginning to fill it in, so that you're clear about what is being asked. (It's a good idea to make a couple of photocopies, and use these as drafts, to avoid sending altered forms.)

If there's no official form, you'll have to prepare your own application, so first make a draft and check that you miss nothing out. You need to:

- set out clearly and concisely the purpose of your project
- state how much money you need and how it will be used
- define the people who will be helped by your project
- state the methods by which you intend to achieve your objectives (a well thought out programme will be a plus factor here)
- show how and at what stages you plan to evaluate your progress
- outline your budget

Enclose any relevant documents, press reports, and so on that will add weight to your case.

Presentation

Your application should be written in clear, concise and unambiguous English, and should be neatly typed. Make sure the addressee's name, title and address are accurate and correctly spelled. Give a contact name and address, so there's no confusion about who should be contacted if further information is needed. Keep photocopies of the application and any other documents sent.

CONTRACTS

If your organisation is or will be providing a service to the community you might be able to negotiate a contract with your local authority (or with another body) to provide that service on their behalf. Service contracts are increasingly replacing grants, and you should familiarise yourself with the implications of this trend. The Directory of Social Change publishes a comprehensive handbook, *Getting Ready for Contracts* by Richard Macfarlane and Sandy Adirondack, which covers all aspects of these new contractual relationships.

5
Help from Industry and Commerce

Industrial and commercial companies can help charities directly in several ways:

- with cash donations
- with gifts in kind
- by sponsorship
- by staff secondment
- by providing services and expertise
- by giving discounts on goods and equipment
- by buying advertising space in programmes, newsletters and so on.

BE SELECTIVE

In his book *Raising Money From Industry*, Michael Norton analyses the results of a 1988 survey which asked companies how and why they responded to charitable appeals. 'Circular appeals' featured strongly among those *least* likely to succeed, so don't waste time and money on this kind of enterprise, however attractive it might look.

Cautionary tale: a group set up to raise funds for renovating a building in a northern town decided they could raise the money in one sweep, with a blanket coverage of UK companies. They sent out 10,000 appeals in the form of a duplicated letter asking for cash donations. The response was nil.

Also according to the survey Michael Norton cites, 85 percent of companies who responded to the questionnaire would not consider responding to 'local appeals with no local relevance or connection to the company.'

With overall company giving in 1991 dropping for the first time in almost a decade despite increasingly favourable tax incentives, it's becoming ever more essential to target those companies most likely to respond to *your* appeal.

Before you approach any company, then, ask yourself:

1. Does the company have a strong local presence, either as a locally based company or as the head office, regional office or prominent local branch of a national or international company?

2. Does the company have a good record of charitable giving and activity? *A Guide to Company Giving* (The Directory of Social Change) gives the relevant details of over 1,300 companies, including their donations policy and who to apply to. *Major Companies and Their Charitable Giving* (The Directory of Social Change) analyses all the relevant aspects of the top 350 companies.

3. Is the company in good financial shape? There's no point in approaching a company that's on the verge of collapse. Local knowledge should keep you in the picture with regard to local companies, and a keen eye on the financial papers should give you a good idea of the position of the larger companies.

4. Do you have or can you make personal contact with top-level staff? 'Who you know' is often the key to a successful approach.

5. Can you establish a 'product link', that is, a mutual interest to link your cause with the company's products or activities? For example, a project setting up a children's play and nursery area could have a very strong appeal for a company making toys, play equipment or children's clothing.

6. Are the company's products and activities compatible with your cause's ethical policies?

Timing
Most companies organise their charitable giving on an annual basis. It will be very useful to find out their budget timetable. Large companies especially take a highly organised attitude to charitable giving, and many have established 'community' departments, with trained staff to handle appeals, allocate funds, arrange secondments and so on. Very few large companies deal with charities on a 'first appeal out of the hat wins' basis.

WHAT DO YOU WANT FROM THEM?

To make an effective appeal, you need to decide exactly what you'll ask for. A vague approach on the lines of

Dear sir, our project is much needed in the community and is worthy of your support. Donations of any kind will be gratefully received'

will be binned straight away. Such an appeal hardly inspires confidence in a group's efficiency, thought and enterprise; it conveys entirely the wrong kind of image.

It's far more effective to draw up a list of everything you need now and envisage needing in the near future, then to ask a company for specific and appropriate help. Even if a company has already allocated its budget for this year, it might put you high on its list for next year if it's impressed by your well thought out and well presented appeal.

Here are just a few suggestions to help you define your own particular list of needs (you'll have already identified at least some of these when you outlined your budget):

- money for specified purposes (to pay for rent, professional services, running expenses); don't be vague — state precise amounts
- office furniture
- paint
- floor covering
- typewriter or word processor
- photocopier
- telephone
- tea urn/coffee machine
- slide projector
- raffle prizes
- stationery
- use of premises (social club, for example) as a venue for an event
- special equipment relevant to your project.

Golden rules for appeal letters.

They should be

1. Written in clear, concise and correct English.

2. Individually typed — *never* duplicated or photocopied.

3. Addressed to a specified and appropriate person.

4. Precise in defining the help requested.

Gifts in kind
A company might be happy to give you, for example:

- office furniture and equipment which are due for replacement
- waste material, seconds, old stock, damaged goods
- discounts on its products or services
- the loan of equipment
- samples of its products to use as raffle prizes.

Secondments
A company might 'lend' you the service of a member of its staff, perhaps full-time for a short period while you're setting up, or part-time in the longer term. (Companies who second staff members to charities are eligible for tax concessions.)

Recommended reading
Raising Money From Industry by Michael Norton (The Directory of Social Change) is a comprehensive guide to raising money and other help from industrial and commercial companies. It gives thoroughly sound and knowledgeable advice on what you can get and how you can get it. Including approaches, examples of how to write effective appeal letters, and case studies, it's packed with illuminating and useful information.

There is useful basic information, too, and leads to further advice in the Directory of Social Change's leaflet *Fund-Raising Sources*.

SOCIAL SPONSORSHIP

Sponsorship in this sense is different from the kind familiar to us all as 'sponsored walks', 'sponsored slims' and so on. Supporting such events commits the 'sponsor' to no more than paying up a previously agreed amount of money per mile walked or pound shed. The 'sponsor' is offered, and expects, nothing in return — he is in effect simply making a cash donation.

Sponsorship by a commercial or industrial company is not the same thing at all, and you need to understand the difference before you decide whether or not business sponsorship is an appropriate means of raising support or money for your cause. Sponsorship from business (often called 'social sponsorship') can be defined as the payment of a fee by a company to a charity (with which the company has no direct connection) in the hope and expectation that the company will benefit from its association with the charity and the charity's activities.

This, then, is a mutually beneficial business arrangement, and it imposes legal obligations on both the company and the charity. These obligations should be defined in an agreement signed by both parties. It's best to have the agreement drawn up (or at least checked) by a solicitor, to be sure that there are no ambiguities in the wording.

It's important to discuss the desirability of seeking sponsorship with your committee and with others on whom you might be depending for support. Some people might be unhappy about taking on the commitments involved. You also need agreement on which companies to approach, if you decide to go ahead. You'll want to avoid applying to any company whose products, policies, practices, research or investments might be inappropriate to your project. If your cause is an environmental one, for example, it could be damaged by association with a company involved in, say, unpopular land development.

Don't underestimate how important this aspect might be. A sponsorship agreement will bind your cause closely to the sponsoring company's name, and if the public perceives that company's activities as being in conflict with or inappropriate to the aims of your cause, no amount of sponsorship money will compensate for the loss of public goodwill. Your integrity is your most valuable asset.

Draw up a list of possible target companies, then investigate them thoroughly. Ask business contacts, read the business and financial papers. Get in touch with other groups with similar ethical views to yours — they might have information they would be willing to share.

You can get information about 'who invests where' from the **Ethical Investment Research Service** (EIRIS), who produce a range of publications including, for example, *The Nuclear Weapons Connection,* a guide to UK companies' links with nuclear weapons. They also publish a quarterly newsletter, *The Ethical Investor.* The company's main clients are investors, both individuals and organisations, and financial advisors who want to make an informed judgement about where money should or should not be invested according to ethical concerns. EIRIS will send you a list of publications and details of their services on request.

WHAT'S IN IT FOR THE SPONSOR?

You know what you want from him — usually money — but what can you offer in return? As Caroline Gillies says in her book *Finding Sponsors for Community Projects* (Directory of Social Change), 90 percent of sponsorship appeals probably fail because 'the proposal is so busy telling the sponsor what the applicant wants that it neglects to tell the potential sponsor what is going to be given in return'.

'More and more organisations are trying to get money out of industry at the moment, so approaches out of the blue are likely to stand less chance than where the company has had some previous contact with an organisation.

'My advice to anyone seeking local sponsorship in particular would be to make friends with local companies *before* you start asking them for funding. Find someone who works for the company and get a bit of background first of all. Why not offer to give talks to their staff on a relevant subject, or training — if appropriate, invite executives to a business lunch and to tour your project, or set up an outing for the social club.

'If you become involved with a company and get to know its staff and executives and show that you're prepared to give as well as take, then your approach for help is going to be received with rather more sympathy.'

Caroline Gillies, Sponsorship Consultant

You need to convince the potential sponsor that the results of his support will be just as valuable to him as to you, if not more so. You can offer, for example:

- extensive publicity through your fund-raising activities
- sales promotion of his products at your events
- access to your mailing list
- introductions to prominent and influential citizens who support your cause
- enhanced prestige and image in the community — the chance to be seen as a 'good citizen' and public benefactor
- media exposure
- his company's name on your stationery, brochures and transport
- cost-effectiveness — it would cost him more to buy the publicity and other benefits than the amount you're asking in sponsorship support.

Work out a sponsorship fee

Put a price on the benefits you're offering. Be specific — and be realistic. You need to strike a reasonable balance between the amount you ask for and the returns you can offer. No company is going to put up £10,000 in return for having its name on a few T-shirts or printed in a newsletter with a readership of 500.

It's best to try for a single sponsorship, too, rather than a piecemeal collection of smaller sums, with all the ensuing administrative complications and possible problems about sponsorship priorities.

Recommended reading

Finding Sponsors for Community Projects: A Step-by-Step Guide by

Ms Dee Tweedle
Managing Director
Mad Hatter Toy Company

Dear Ms Tweedle

We are a local group setting up a new project, a play centre for children under five living in our community. The project will be based in the old church hall at St Michael's, Pond Lane. (The church building itself is now used by the Shakybridge Society of Arts, Crafts and Literature, who are leasing the church hall to us.)

Our project might be of interest to you as an opportunity to promote your products through a sponsorship arrangement. We can offer a variety of sponsorship methods to suit your budget, for example

1.   Toys and play equipment: our project would use *only* 'Mad Hatter' products, while you supply the toys and equipment on an on-going basis with replacements as necessary. Prominent publicity would be given to this fact in all our promotional material, such as brochures, events programmes, publicity leaflets and advertising.

2.   Programme advertising: we would reserve for you a full-page back cover advertising space in every event programme (a minimum of 6 per year) at a cost of £100 per event, or £150 to include a front cover flash and promotion in the editorial content.

3.   Product popularity testing: we would provide a facility for your company to conduct popularity tests on current and new products during our regular opening hours, at a cost of £50 – £100 per product depending on the type and duration of the tests.

4.   We would feature your company name and logo on promotional merchandise to be sold at our centre and at events, at a cost to you, for example, of £50 per 1,000 ball point pens, £60 per 1,000 printed balloons, £250 per 5,000 printed prize draw tickets. . . Other items will be available.

5.   Your name and logo featured on two display boards, one at the gate to the grounds, the other on the exterior wall of the hall, at a cost of £200 per board per annum. (Both boards will be in unmissable view of all visitors to the Arts Centre and to our hall.)

Perhaps you have other ideas you would like to discuss with us. One of the mutual benefits of sponsorship is its great flexibility. Could we arrange a meeting to discuss ideas?

Yours sincerely

Eric Gogetter
Fund-raising coordinator
Peter Pan Play Project

Figure 6. Example of a letter applying for sponsorship.

Caroline Gillies (Directory of Social Change). This invaluable guide for organisations seeking social sponsorship is written by a practising sponsorship consultant. It takes you through all the procedures required for success, and includes all the practical advice and examples you'll need, presented in a clear, easy to follow layout and down-to-earth style.

Following six very successful years as Watford Football Club's Marketing Manager, Caroline Gillies now runs First Division Marketing, a consultancy specialising in environmental, tourism and sports sponsorship. Caroline operates her sponsorship consultancy on a rather unusual basis with a network of freelance consultants whose specialist skills are used as appropriate for each client. Her method is not to charge a hefty percentage for finding a sponsor but to set the sponsor-seeking organisation on the right path for helping itself. 'A few days of our time and advice at the outset is a good long-term investment for a community organisation,' she says, 'because then it learns how to market itself, rather than relying on outsiders.'

Action Match

Action Match is a national agency devoted to promoting and supporting the development of social sponsorship. Its development programme

- promotes the idea of social sponsorship
- helps both businesses and charities make social sponsorship work for them
- encourages the development of good practice.

Action Match organises events and training programmes, and publishes practical booklets and a quarterly magazine, all available to members. (One of their recent booklets is *Social Sponsorship in Action*, sponsored by Allied Dunbar.)

At the time of going to press, membership of Action Match is £8 per annum to voluntary organisations, £16 to companies. They'll send you details of membership and of activities and publications on request.

You'll also find some very useful advice, along with application examples, in The Directory of Social Change leaflet *Social Sponsorship*.

6
Keep It Legal

There are legal restrictions governing how you can raise money from the public. Charity Commission leaflet CC20 *Fund Raising and Charities* outlines the basic statutory provisions controlling fund-raising, and you can find information on legal requirements and good practice in *Voluntary but Not Amateur* (London Voluntary Service Council). The National Council for Voluntary Organisations (Bedford Square Press) publishes *But is it legal? Fundraising and the law* by Sally Capper.

Here are some guidelines, and if you would like further advice, perhaps on a specific event, contact your local authority.

LOTTERIES AND RAFFLES

The law distinguishes three main types of lottery:

- small lotteries
- private lotteries
- society lotteries

Whether you need a licence depends on which type of lottery you plan to hold. If you're in any doubt at all about this, consult the appropriate licencing or registration authority. These are:

1. The appropriate local district or borough council

2. The Common Council of the City of London

3. In the Metropolitan Police District, the Commission of Police.

The **Gaming Board for Great Britain** will advise you about restrictions on prizes, expenses, ticket pricing, minimum age of participants and so on.

The types of lottery

1. Small lotteries
These are the raffles, tombolas and similar types of lottery held at events like fetes, bazaars, coffee mornings. The total value of the prizes must not exceed £50, and the proceeds (after deduction of expenses) must not be used for any kind of private gain. No cash prizes may be offered, and all ticket sales must be carried out on the premises and during the entertainment, as must the announcement of the results.

2. Private lotteries
These are lotteries in which tickets are sold only to people living or working in the same premises, or to members of a society, institution,

---

No. 0101   Sponsored by Mad Hatter Toys   No. 0101

GRAND CHRISTMAS PRIZE DRAW

In aid of The Peter Pan Play Project

To be drawn: 16th December 1992

at St. Michael's Hall

Prizes

1. Portable colour TV and video recorder
2. Microwave oven
3. Radio cassette
4. Picture quilt for double bed

Plus   25 other prizes including turkeys, wine and Christmas
         puddings and cakes.

Promoter: E.B. Gogetter
c/o Peter Pan Play Project, Pond Land, Shakybridge

Printed by George Inckman & Co,
High Street,   Registered Charity No. oxoxoxo
Shakybridge   Licence No. xyz123

Figure 7. Example of prize draw ticket.

association or club. You can only deduct printing and stationery expenses, and all remaining proceeds must be used for the purposes of the society or for the provision of prizes.

3. Society lotteries
Odd though the designation might seem, these are public lotteries, and are limited to 52 per organisation in any one year, at intervals of not less than seven days. Such lotteries must be registered with the appropriate authority (see above). Lotteries where the value of tickets sold is more than £10,000, or where the value of the largest prize is more than £2,000, must also be registered with the Gaming Board for Great Britain.

Your 'society lottery'
If you want to run a raffle in aid of your cause on a larger scale than those held at a fete or other specific event, this would come under the designation of a society lottery. You need to get special tickets printed that are only valid for this event. The tickets should bear the name of your organisation and its charity registration number, a list of the prizes offered, the ticket price, and the licence number allocated by the appropriate authority. The date and place of the draw should be prominently printed. The name and address of the printer should also appear on the ticket.

STREET COLLECTIONS AND FLAG DAYS

These are subject to local regulations which may vary from one authority to another. It's essential that you consult the relevant authority before attempting to raise money in public places. Regulations cover matters like avoiding traffic obstruction, avoiding unacceptable methods of collecting money, whether or not articles may be sold in public places in aid of your charity and so on.

Your local authority will allocate you a specific day on which no other organisation will be allowed to put collectors on the streets, and will provide the required permit. Saturday is by far the best day, but you might have to wait for as long as a year for this. Get your application in as early as possible.

What about house to house collections?
You must not make house to house collections without a licence, or without an exemption from the requirement to have a licence. This regulation also covers visits from one place of business to another, for

example going round the local pubs, and the selling of articles on the basis that part of the proceeds will be used for charitable purposes.

PRINTED MATERIAL

Every piece of printed material — brochures, leaflets, prize draw tickets, programmes — must have an imprint, that is the names and addresses of the printer and the publisher or promoter. The printer must keep a copy for his records, including a note of who commissioned the work.

Material distributed to the public must not be obscene, indecent or profane or likely to cause racial tension.

TOYS

Toys offered for sale must comply with European Community (EC) safety regulations. Your local **Trading Standards Office** will supply free of charge a copy of the booklet *The Single Market: Toy Safety*, plus any specific local regulations. (Some authorities enforce more stringent regulations than others.) In general, observe the following guidelines:

1. **Soft toys** must be made from non-flammable material and filled with non-flammable stuffing. Make this requirement clear to anyone who offers to make or contribute soft toys. Toy-making materials and stuffing can be tested by putting a lighted match to a small sample. Discard anything that flares up or melts. If washing or dry-cleaning might affect the safety of the toy, it must be clearly labelled 'Do not wash or dry-clean'.

If any of your band of toy-makers can't afford to buy the necessary materials, perhaps you could supply them from a contingency fund set up for such purposes. Suppliers of British Standard approved materials advertise regularly in magazines like *Popular Crafts*. (It's much cheaper to buy in bulk. For example a polyester filling bought in 6lb packs costs £1.50 per lb, but bought in 50lb packs it costs about £1.10 per lb.)

Recycled fabric and yarn can be used, as long as they are washed and comply with the safety regulations.

Facial features made of glass, plastic, wood, metal or other non-pliable material must be of the 'safety' kind which can be attached so that they can't be gripped by a child's fingers or teeth, or pulled off without a force being used which is beyond a child's strength — defined as a force of 20.21 lbs.

For toys intended for very young children, it's best to embroider the features, making sure no loose ends of thread or wool are accessible.

Check that all components are very firmly sewn together so that small fingers can't pull out scraps of stuffing. Check that knitted toys are not made from fabrics whose patterns have holes or gaps knitted into them.

2. **Hygiene:** toys must be made to high standards of cleanliness and hygiene, avoiding any risk of infection or contamination.

3. **Paint:** any paints used must comply with the safety regulations, especially with regard to lead content.

4. **Electrically operated toys:** toys operated on mains electricity must not need a voltage higher than 24, and must have a separate control unit or transformer.

5. **Metal and wood toys:** these must be free of sharp edges and sharply pointed wires, rods or spikes.

6. **Packaging:** toys must not be packaged in thin plastic film. Any plastic film used must be thick enough not be a danger to a child who might pull it over his or her head.

FOOD AND DRINK

The regulations on selling food and drink are mainly concerned with hygiene, for example:

● all equipment must be kept clean
● servers' hands and clothing must be clean
● cuts or grazes must be covered with waterproof dressings
● each stall must have a covered rubbish bin
● food should be kept covered until sold
● containers and wrappings must be clean and without risk of contaminating food
● no toilet should open directly on to a room where food is being sold or served.

Detailed regulations are available from your local authority environmental health department.

Licensing laws
It's pretty easy to get an occasional licence to run a bar at a function; apply

to the local authority (usually the local licensing magistrates) at least one month before your event. An organisation won't be allowed more than four licences per licensing area per year.

Getting permission to run a regular bar is not so easy. Your local authority will advise you.

Remember that it's an offence to sell alcohol to anyone under 18.

Charity Commission Leaflet *CC27, The Provision of Alcohol on Charity Premises*, gives outline information, and advises that you consult your legal adviser or the Commissioners to make sure there's no risk of committing an offence, particularly when alcohol is to be sold rather than simply consumed. There could be taxation as well as legal complications.

MUSIC

Contact **The Performing Right Society** for permission to perform or play recordings of music. (Permission fees are often waived for charities.)

INSURANCE

The type and amount of insurance you need — and you'll certainly need some — depends on what kind of organisation you are, what kind of premises you have and what your activities are. You should take advice from an insurance company experienced in charity work. Contact the **British Insurance Brokers Association** for advice on finding appropriate companies. It's essential to get the right advice. You can't afford to risk heavy liabilities, or to pay high premiums for inadequate or inappropriate cover.

One aspect often overlooked by fund-raising groups is that participation in certain activities on the group's behalf can sometimes invalidate personal insurances. Be sure to get qualified advice on this.

7
Some Inspiration. . . And Some Advice

In this and the chapters that follow we'll look in detail at some fund-raising activities, with expert advice on running them. First, though, here's a tale of inspiration.

NOT SUCH A WILD IDEA

Occasionally a fund-raiser hits on an idea that seems at the same time brilliant and unlikely to work. If such an idea strikes you, don't laugh at your over-active imagination — try it.

On the day HRH The Prince of Wales broke his arm playing polo, Reginald and Sheila Little happened to drive past the hospital the Prince was rushed to from the field. The throng of press and police caught their attention.

Mr and Mrs Little were in the area quite by chance, responding to a family crisis. Reginald Little is Warden of St Thomas of Canterbury Church in Kingswear, Devon, and fund-raising was much on his mind at this time. The roof of his church desperately needed repair after the violent storms of 1989. As he settled down to sleep that night, an idea flashed into his mind: what if he were to ask Prince Charles to donate his plaster cast to be raffled in aid of the church roof repair appeal? His wife told him he was 'completely crackers' — he wouldn't stand a chance.

In the morning, however, Mr Little talked over the idea with his son and they decided it was worth a try. They composed a careful letter, mentioning the Prince's connection with Dartmouth, just across the River Dart from the church, and also that St Thomas of Canterbury is a Crown Living. At nearby Highgrove they could find no letterbox so they tossed the letter over the gates, more or less abandoning hope of a favourable response even if someone found the letter before the elements destroyed it.

They were proved wrong. Within a week a letter from St James's Palace advised them that in principle His Royal Highness would be entirely happy to donate his plaster cast to such a worthy cause. The letter requested that there should be no publicity until the cast was ready for collection, just in case it disintegrated on removal or was otherwise rendered unavailable. The Littles didn't breathe a word for ten nail-biting days, until they picked up the binbag-wrapped cast from Highgrove.

As soon as he got back to Kingswear Mr Little began organising the raffle. At first the public, residents and tourists alike, were sceptical — was the cast authentic? The letters from the palace had to be produced and the story told time and time again, so Mr Little and his helpers had posters printed explaining the enterprise, and the word began to spread. They amassed 34 additional good prizes, and the raffle raised a highly satisfactory £17,000.

The Right Reverend Peter Coleman, Bishop of Crediton, made the draw in October 1990, and the cast was won by Mrs Schofield, who had bought her ticket while on holiday from the Colchester area. By coincidence, another visitor from that area was present at the draw and offered to deliver the prize, which travelled in a specially made glass-fronted mahogany case. With it went its authenticating letters.

The royal trophy's arrival drew an army of photographers and reporters. A television company even sent a helicopter to get a report and interview back in time for evening viewing. Mrs Schofield became something of a celebrity, much in demand for interviews for magazines from all over the world. Such is the power of a royal connection.

But that wasn't the end of the story. It was picked up by the national press, and many people recalled holidays in the Kingswear and Dartmouth area. Quite a few had some connections with St Thomas of Canterbury — weddings, baptisms and so on — but many more responded to the sheer novelty of the idea. Donations poured in. Over seven months, the appeal drew the remarkable total of £46,000, a sum beyond Mr Little's wildest dreams.

'My advice to anyone would be that if they get a seemingly way-out idea, at least to try for it as people can only say no, and they might say yes!'
Reginald Little, Church Warden,
St Thomas of Canterbury Church, Kingswear, Devon

Top fund-raiser

According to recent newspaper reports, the Prince of Wales is the world's top fund-raiser, with donations to his charities reaching more than £124 million. Prince Charles's single biggest coup, it's reported, was to persuade the government to match, pound for pound, the money raised through his Youth Business Trust. This has so far cost the government more than £40 million.

CELEBRITY ATTRACTIONS

What special attraction is guaranteed to bring crowds of people to your event? Experienced fund-raisers would answer in two words: a celebrity. From *Coronation Street* or Manchester United, from the BBC *Newsdesk* or *Top of the Pops*, a famous face with a famous name is a sure-fire crowd-puller. (If you're on nodding terms with royalty, however minor, and can persuade them to put in even a brief appearance, you'll break attendance records.)

What if I don't know a celebrity?
If you don't know anyone famous personally, where do you find your celebrity? And won't the cost wipe out your profits?

Over to Sal Keegan: Sal is a seasoned organiser of fund-raising events, with an impressive list of successes to her credit. She has staged such events as a Three Day Horse Trial which included a musical ride in which television stars rode the horses of famous show-jumpers; a boating regatta; variety shows; quiz nights; dog and pet shows; fetes and fairs and dozens more.

That horse show, incidentally, was held to raise funds for the Lifeboats charity. Why horses? That was a piece of original thinking that added an extra dimension of interest to the event: in its early days, the lifeboat service relied on horses to pull the boats down to the sea.

Sal's energy and know-how are currently focused on raising money to establish a conservatory day-room at St Ann's Hospice, Little Hulton, Salford. The conservatory will be a memorial to her late husband, Robert Keegan, well remembered as a popular star of television's *Z-Cars*.

'Big events take a lot of forward planning,' Sal advises. 'You need at least 12 months to stage an outdoor event like a summer fete.' Sal prefers to do all the planning herself, working as a 'committee of one' and organising appropriate help for the day of the event. She has found that over-60s clubs are always happy to help with jobs that are not too physically demanding, like selling raffle tickets or taking money on the door.

Sal runs Pancho Promotions, an agency specialising in 'Television Star Names Personal Appearances and Advertising'. A star name can cost from around £500 to £10,000. You can't afford that kind of money? With a bit of thought and imagination, you don't have to.

How can we pay for a celebrity?
As Sal says, you can have your celebrity for a fraction of those costs (and maybe for nothing at all) if you can find a company to sponsor your star's appearance. Thought and imagination are key elements of any successful fund-raising project, of course, and they can pay spectacular dividends here. Sal offers an example: if there is a large bakery firm in your area, ask them if they would sponsor a star from the TV series *Bread*. Prepare your approach carefully, so that you can present the company with a convincing argument that their investment will be worthwhile. (See the section on Social Sponsorship in Chapter 5.)

Your sponsorship proposal should include evidence that you've thought up plenty of activities that will entice the press to attend — it's essential that your prospective sponsor knows that he'll benefit from extensive press coverage both before and after the event. In this case, for example, you could suggest as one of your attractions a stall where you soak bread rolls (stale ones supplied by your sponsor) till they go soft and soggy; persuade the vicar to sit in the stocks and invite the crowd to pay for the privilege of pelting him with the squishy rolls. They'll love it. A stall like this will give your sponsor a chance to erect a large advertising sign, and the novelty of setting up the vicar (or any other local dignitary) for target practice will offer a great photo opportunity that includes exposure of the sponsor's name.

More sponsorship ideas
Here are just a few more suggestions for appropriate sponsorship, to start you thinking:

● a brewery to sponsor a star from *Coronation Street* or *EastEnders*
● a record company or recording studio to sponsor a musician or pop star
● a printing company or publisher to sponsor an author
● a sports' clothing or equipment company to sponsor a sporting star.

Good press coverage serves more than one purpose. Not only will your sponsor see that his investment has bought him favourable publicity, and contributed to the desirable image of being a 'good citizen', but the public beyond your immediate area (possibly far beyond it) will read about your cause. And this could bring you unexpected support.

Sal Keegan tells of her own recent experience of this plus factor: a write-up about her Conservatory Appeal caught the attention of a local building company which had just held a Sportsman Dinner. They sent Sal a cheque for £2,500, money raised at the dinner. And things didn't stop there. To show her appreciation of such a generous donation, Sal arranged for three TV stars to accept the cheque at a small ceremony. She didn't have to pay the stars — they were appearing in a play at the local theatre, and when Sal told them about the cheque they not only agreed to come along to the presentation but also visited the hospice, to the surprise and delight of the patients and staff. The resulting publicity was a bonus for the building company, and it was very good for Sal's appeal, both financially and in terms of public goodwill. It also led to Sal's being asked to contribute to this book.

'Think big and think different,' Sal says. You can make money quickly with small events, but it's the bigger ones that will get the publicity.

Forward planning

Bear in mind that popular stars are busy stars, and are often tied up with filming and touring commitments for a long time ahead. You need to allow plenty of time, so start planning well before your event. Get a list of possible names from an entertainment agency like Sal's, remember to ask about fees both for the star's services and the agency's, and keep in close touch with the agent. He or she will help you find the right person for *your* event, at a fee that will be acceptable for sponsorship or part-sponsorship, according to the possible sponsorship benefits you'll be able to offer. This is a point you shouldn't disregard. You'll be wasting everybody's time, besides courting financial disaster, if you engage a celebrity at a fee of, say, £2,500 to open a garden party where you can only accommodate 50 or 60 invited guests. It would be unrealistic to expect any sponsor to see that as beneficial to his company, and the event couldn't possibly raise enough to cover such a cost.

Arranging sponsorship will usually be your responsibility. It's well worth whatever effort it takes. At an event that might normally attract 500 people, a celebrity presence could bring 5,000 through the gate. And if you give them plenty to enjoy when they get there, they'll stay, and they'll spend.

> Plan every detail. It won't come right on the night unless it is planned down to the smallest detail. Don't leave anything to chance.
>
> Sal Keegan

LIVE MUSIC

How do I plan a live music event?

To help you plan an event where you'll want live music, here are some guidelines from Johnny Howard Associates, one of the country's top entertainment agencies:

Reputable agencies
Most reputable agencies are members of the **Entertainment Agents Association**, and conduct their business ethically. The agency you book through tries to ensure that an engagement is fulfilled satisfactorily, but takes no responsibility in the case of a default. The agency has no obligation apart from arranging the booking.

Booking
There are no set rules governing how far ahead you should book, but on average bookings should be made three to six months in advance. A specific big-name band or artist might have to be booked earlier.

Contracts
A written contract is essential, setting out details of the venue, date, time, fees and any other agreed conditions. The contract is between the organiser and the band or artist, and both parties are responsible for fulfilling the terms agreed.

Facilities
The organiser is expected to provide adequate facilities such as convenient parking, changing-room(s) if appropriate, toilet access and so on, and it's usual to provide light refreshments for the musicians and artists, too. This should be clarified in advance.

How big a band?
This depends on the type of function and the capacity of the venue. If you're at all unsure about this, take advice from the agent or the venue.

Costs
Average fees in 1991 were £450 for a four-piece band/group, £1,000 for an eight-piece, and for a well known big band of about 13 musicians, around £1,750/£2,000, all plus VAT at current rates.

The music
The musical programme can be decided in various ways. A good band-leader can assess the type of engagement and play an appropriate programme, but some organisers prefer to contact the leader in advance

and either discuss the programme or specify what they require. (Volume is often a contentious point.)

Performing Rights
The venue is responsible for clearing the licensing required from the **Performing Right Society**.

Playing time
Normally a band/group plays for about three hours with a half-hour break midway. If your event extends beyond midnight, you'll have to pay increased rates as specified by the **Musicians Union** — approximately 50 per cent more than before midnight.

Sound systems
A band/group normally provides its own sound system, but if you're booking cabaret artists you'll usually have to provide a sound system as required by the artists.

Insurance
The bandleader should have employees protection insurance, and the venue should also have accident and public liability cover. You might want to check these points.

A big show

If your ambitions run to a big musical show with a top show band, you'll have to budget for bigger fees than those quoted above. For example, you could book The Glenn Miller Orchestra UK, which consists of 19 personnel including vocalists plus two sound crew. (Many orchestras in the UK play Miller-style music, but this is the only one licensed by the Miller Estate in New York.) The orchestra's director, John Watson, lays on a show which covers the original Miller orchestra's music from 1938 through to 1944, the year of Glenn's never-explained disappearance. The programme includes the re-creation of Glenn's civilian band and army band, complete with uniforms. The full evening's entertainment will cost you from around £3,500.

Equity

Professional actors, television personalities, cabaret artistes and singers are members of Equity, The British Actors Equity Association. If you want to contact a particular personality, Equity can give you the name and address of his or her agent.

8
Running a Charity Shop

Charity shops, sometimes called 'thrift shops', earn many thousands of pounds every year for international, national and local charities. You can usually find at least one such shop in most high streets. A strategically sited and well run shop could be very profitable for *your* cause, too.

If you are a registered charity selling goods which are mostly or entirely donated, you would qualify for **rate relief**. The new business rate now applies, and as this is much higher than the old rate, rate relief is even more welcome. How much relief you would get depends largely on current legislation and could vary from one local authority to another. The Imperial Cancer Research Shop in Altrincham for example (see below) receives an 80 per cent mandatory reduction from its local authority.

You need to find premises within your means, of course, but you shouldn't let the prospect of very low rent and rates be the deciding factor. There's little point in setting up in dingy premises in a back street in an under-populated area. You would be throwing money away — how many people would bother to go looking for you? Look, rather, for unlet shops, or premises scheduled for redevelopment, in a busy shopping street where you'll get plenty of passing trade.

If you spot a vacant shop displaying an agent's board, approach the agent as well as your local authority. If there is no board, go direct to the local authority, who should be able to put you in touch with the property owners. You need to know:

- if you could use the premises, and for how long
- if you can afford them, taking concessions into account
- if basic services like water and power are available
- if the premises are hygienic, vermin-free, and have adequate toilet facilities
- if the premises can be made secure without too much expense.

A sympathetic owner might waive rental charges altogether on a short lease. You could suggest a mutually beneficial sponsorship deal — see the section on Social Sponsorship in Chapter 5.

Joyce Kenworthy manages the Imperial Cancer Research Fund's shop in Altrincham, Cheshire. From her years of practical experience of the job — a job, incidentally, that is entirely voluntary — Joyce advises that you look particularly at the following points.

LOCATION

A good location is absolutely essential. The ICRF shop in Altrincham is ideally situated just a few yards from the railway and bus stations. Pedestrians heading for the main shopping precinct and the town's busy market pass directly in front of the shop window and door. This is a very advantageous site, and while you might not be lucky enough to find anything quite that good, you should certainly avoid any location where the pedestrian flow is sparse.

SAFETY

When you find premises you think would be suitable, you must have them checked for safety and security, as well as ensuring that the necessary services are laid on. You need to arrange visits from your local **Fire Prevention** and **Crime Prevention Officers**, and also from your insurance company. These specialists will advise you on such vital matters as fire safety, how to make the premises secure, how to make sure there are accessible and clearly marked emergency exits and so on.

STAFF

You'll need enough helpers to keep your shop open during regular hours, however limited. Joyce's shop is open all day every day from Monday to Saturday. She tries to have a minimum of four people manning the shop at every session, three in the shop and one or two working behind the scenes.

How many workers?

Most volunteers work one or two sessions a week, either mornings or afternoons. With 12 sessions a week and four people per session, assuming one session per volunteer per week, you would need about 50 people to make a six-day opening possible. And if your town has particularly busy shopping days, as Altrincham does on Tuesdays and Saturdays when its large and popular market is open all day, you'll probably want extra hands in the shop. If your present support is not enough to allow so many helpers, organise your shop opening to cover either shorter hours or a limited number of days per week. The important thing is to be open at regular times.

Joyce doesn't close her shop at lunchtime, which is often the busiest time for trade. Her volunteers work on a rota system, with complete teams changing over in the middle of the day.

ICRF hold training meetings before a new shop is opened, so that inexperienced volunteers can get hands-on practice at the till, learn the pricing system, see how to sort donated goods and so on. New volunteers then spend two or three sessions working with the manager or with an experienced helper before they undertake a regular session in the shop.

Who should work there?

You need to apply some degree of selectivity when making up your teams of volunteers. Hard though it might be to turn down *any* offer of help, shop workers need to be at least reasonably fit physically, especially if there are stairs on your premises. A volunteer who has problems moving about or carrying stock could cause an unfair amount of work to fall on others on the rota, and this in turn could lead to resentment and even to the loss of a strong, hard-working volunteer.

The main qualities your helpers need are:

● commitment to your cause
● reliability
● tolerance, patience, and the ability to deal firmly with the occasional awkward customer
● a strong sense of humour — perhaps the most important quality of all, especially needed when things go wrong.

STOCK

All the stock sold in ICRF shops is donated. Nothing is bought in. Ask your helpers and other supporters to spread the word that you are looking for stock. A short editorial item, or a letter to the editor in your local paper should bring some results, especially if you can offer a collection service in the area. Include a contact number, and also give details about the hours your shop will be open so that people can bring goods along. All this information can also be included in any leaflets you hand out or have in the shop.

Be selective with your stock. Don't refuse to take anything (unless it's downright dirty or potentially dangerous) but set a reasonably high standard for the goods you'll offer in your shop, and make sure your helpers are aware of the standard you want to maintain. Don't throw anything away, though. A rag merchant will be happy to take rejected clothing off your hands, and should give you a small fee for it. There are also dealers who will take other unwanted items, perhaps as a job lot. Look for such merchants and dealers in *Yellow Pages*. If your shop is to be a fairly long-term enterprise, it's worth establishing an on-going arrangement whereby a dealer will make a regular collection call.

WINDOW DISPLAY

Your window display is second only in importance to your location. You want people to stop and look, to like what they see, and to be tempted into your shop. Give your window-dressing as much thought and care as it takes to make it look as professional and attractive as any 'commercial' shop. A theme based on a single colour can be particularly effective. Yellow is especially eye-catching, even from some distance away, and has been proved to draw people across the street to take a closer look.

What will make it even more appealing?
Avoid clutter. Two or three garments imaginatively displayed, with a few complementary accessories, make a far stronger visual impact than a random variety of goods. Avoid, too, putting notices, posters and so on in your window.

Think up ways to tie your display in with what is currently happening in your area. If your town holds a festival, for example, your window could reflect the festival theme. Seasonal events, too, offer opportunities for interesting and imaginative displays. With a bit of flair and imagination, you could make your shop window a focus of local interest which people watch to see what new ideas you're coming up with.

INSIDE THE SHOP

Display your stock as far as possible on the lines of a conventional shop. Much will depend on how much space you have, but you should do your best to make your shop as attractive and pleasant as possible.

Sort clothing into categories and sizes, and put as much as you can on hangers. It's a great help if some of your volunteers are willing to do a bit of spot-cleaning and laundering, so that everything looks and smells as fresh as possible. Keep the shop well ventilated, and use air-freshener if necessary; used clothing in an airless atmosphere has a particularly distinctive smell which can be very off-putting.

Try to find hobbyists who will look through items like bric-a-brac, books, pictures, old toys, stamps and so on, in case someone has given you something that you could sell to a specialist dealer. They would give you far more than you would get by selling the item in the shop. Display bric-a-brac and other small items on shelves, not in jumbled heaps. Arrange books, also on shelves if possible, so that their spines are facing outward and their titles easily seen.

Pricing

ICRF shops price their stock according to a set range of prices. Each session's team of helpers has a 'pricer' who is responsible for deciding which price band each item should be placed in. There is no haggling — the item is either sold at the marked price or it stays in its place. There are no 'sales', in the sense that other shops sell stock off at bargain prices every so often. In ICRF shops, the item is displayed at the price decided for one month. It's then offered for one week at half price. If it still doesn't sell, it's taken out of stock and passed over to a dealer as a reject. This method keeps the stock turning over, and regular customers know that they won't be looking at the same old stock week after week.

It's important to get your pricing policy right. Common sense plus a bit of research around other well-run charity shops should enable you to set your prices at the right level for the quality of the goods you offer. There will inevitably be customers who complain that your prices are far too high, but if you've really thought through your pricing and made fair decisions about it, you can refute these claims with confidence.

Always remember that your sole purpose in running the shop is to raise money for your cause. You are not in the business of providing goods for the public to carry off at give-away prices. It isn't unknown for individuals who dress shabbily and plead imminent destitution as they do the rounds of charity shops to turn up at smart antique and collectors' fairs selling their bargains at substantial profit.

Cash and stock security

Shoplifting is a constant problem. Staff need to be on the alert all the time. Thieves develop ingenious ways of walking off with stock, especially clothing. Don't be surprised to find a mucky old pair of shoes where someone has found a better pair and left the shop while wearing them.

The till should be placed where it's in clear view from anywhere in the shop. In ICRF shops, each team cashes up at the end of its session, before handing over to the next team. In this way, each team takes responsibility for its handling of that session's takings. This method also gives each team the satisfaction of knowing how profitable its session has been.

Other benefits

As well as raising substantial sums, a well run popular shop can bring other benefits. It can:

- keep your cause's name visible in the community
- provide the public with information about your cause and its activities
- attract additional active support as well as donations
- put volunteers in contact with each other. Many people who give time to a regular stint in a charity shop find that they form lasting friendships with other volunteers, thus enriching their own lives while helping the cause.

Far afield

The people who come into your shop can spread the word over surprising distances. Joyce mentions a letter she received from an English lady living in Angoulême, France, whose daughter had told her about the ICRF shop. The lady wrote offering to send knitted goods and asking what kind of things would be most suitable. By pure coincidence, on the same day a customer came in looking for tea-cosies. A correspondence developed, the lady in France supplied the customer's needs, and also contributed some beautifully made baby clothes. Little incidents like this add spice to the work, and encourage helpers and customers alike.

9
Outdoor Events

Flag days, fetes, festivals, fun-runs, fairs. . . the scope for outdoor fund-raising is as wide as your imagination and enterprise. Whatever your event, meticulous planning and detailed preparation are the keys to success, as ever. Many of the organising principles outlined in the following pages are relevant to almost any outdoor occasion. Adapt them to suit your own events.

A STREET COLLECTION

The amount you raise from your street collection/flag day will be in direct proportion to the number of people out there collecting on your behalf, so you need to rally as many collectors as you possibly can. Don't expect any collector to do more than two hours at a stretch, especially in bad weather. (There will always be a few stalwarts who'll insist on doing longer, but don't let them bully other people into thinking they must do the same.)

Inform the police that you have the necessary **permit** — they need to know that *your* collectors and no others have permission to be out collecting.

Issue every collector with a **badge** and an **identifying certificate**, both of which should carry the collector's name and be signed by the organiser. Tins or boxes must be sealed and numbered, and you should keep a record of which collector takes out which number tin(s).

Etiquette
Make sure all your collectors understand the legal obligations and the etiquette of collecting in public places. They must not ask for money or block people's path or shake cans in people's faces or behave in any way that could be held to be intimidating. Complaints from the public could lead to difficulties with the police and the local authority, and could count against you next time you seek permits or licences. Aggressive behaviour

also presents your cause in a bad light, and could undo much of the hard work you're putting into building up your image and goodwill.

A friendly smile and a big 'Thank you' to everyone who contributes will gain more goodwill (and money) than a pushy approach.

Planning your approach
You need:

- A central headquarters from which you direct operations, allocate tins and badges, and to which full cans are returned.

- An up-to-date large-scale local street map on which you pin-point suitable collecting areas and places where collectors can deliver tins at the end of their stint if they are outside easy walking distance of headquarters; arrange for someone with a vehicle to be there at certain times — not all your helpers will have cars at their disposal.

- All the necessary equipment — tins, badges and so on — plus plenty of tea and coffee to provide your 'troops' with sustenance.

- People — the most essential element.

On your map, highlight key areas like busy shopping streets and malls, supermarkets and other large stores. The latter two might give you permission to station collectors at entrances and exits on their private property. It's especially useful to have permission to stand inside store foyers if the weather is bad. People will be a lot more ready to stop and dig out a few coins if they're under cover. You must be able to assure such a sympathetic manager that his doorways won't be blocked or his customers harassed.

Bus and railway stations are good spots, but again you might need permission, depending on which areas are public and which belong to British Rail or the bus companies.

Your accountability
All the money you collect must be seen to be accounted for. Your local authority might require you to return a form listing the amounts collected in each can, together with the name of the collector, within a given time. Check this.

All the returned tins should be opened in the presence of the organiser plus at least one other person, and the amount from each tin recorded and witnessed.

You should make arrangements for the money to be safely deposited in a bank or other safe place as soon as your collection is complete. Ask a local bank to advise you.

Your publicity

Ask the local press and radio to announce your collection as near the day as possible, urging people to give generously. After the event, announce the amount of money raised, thanking everybody who donated and everybody who helped. Take the opportunity to remind readers and listeners of what the money will be used for — this might bring in a few more donations.

Good relations

Try to write to every individual who helped. This is time-consuming, but it's a wonderful investment in future help. People like to feel valued.

Cautionary tale

Don't try to be too clever. One nationally known (and very worthy) organisation recently held a 'flag' day on which they offered an emblem brooch to donors who gave £1 or more to their cause. Unfortunately, by far the most prominent words on their collecting boxes were 'Minimum donation £1'. You had to look very closely to see that this referred to receiving one of the brooches, and not directly to the amount people were expected to give. Many of the boxes were displayed on checkout counters, ideal for dropping small change into them — but most people passing through read those words and put the coins back in their pockets or purses with comments like 'What a cheek!' or 'I can't afford a pound, so they can't have anything'.

A DONKEY DERBY

For a crowd-pulling attraction you can't beat a Donkey Derby. Provided you put in enough effort beforehand, even bad weather and a disappointing turnout won't stop you making a profit.

David Allott has specialised in Donkey Derbys for over 30 years, and has helped charitable organisations raise millions of pounds. Mr Allott and his donkeys travel all over the north-east of England — anywhere within a day's round trip from their base in Knaresborough. He charges according to the number of donkeys supplied, the distance travelled and the transport costs involved.

A Donkey Derby is a sure money-maker, he says. How much you make depends on how much work you put into it. Here's David Allott's recipe for a great family fun day and a fund-raising triumph.

Preparation tips

You need team work, with as many people as possible selling race sponsorship, donkey 'ownership', advertising space in your programme, then organising publicity and selling programmes in advance. Here's how to do it:

1. First book your donkeys. There are not as many donkey teams in the UK today as there used to be, and there's a limited number of weeks in the year when you might reasonably hope for good weather, so advance booking is essential. A year ahead is not too long, especially for weekends.

2. Book your venue. Look for a privately owned field, school playing field, sports ground and so on — you can't charge for entrance to public land.

3. Start selling the following as early as possible:

●   Sponsorship of the races themselves, for a flat fee. What you charge depends on the scale of your event and the amount of publicity the race sponsors are likely to get, but around £30 is usual. In return, the sponsors' names are prominently displayed in the programme/race-card, thus promoting goodwill and possibly business too.

●   'Ownership' of a donkey. There are usually eight races on the card, with eight donkeys in each race. 'Ownership' is sold at, say, £10 per donkey, and the owner chooses his donkey's name for that race.

●   Advertising space in the programme. It's best to keep the divisions of space simple, perhaps offering whole, half or quarter pages. Smaller ads tend to complicate the laying out of the pages. Charge a little more pro rata for quarter and half pages, say £10 per whole page, £6 per half page and £3.50 per quarter page. You'll have to judge for yourselves what level of rates you could reasonably ask for your particular event.

Don't leave all the selling to one or two people. You want as much cash in the kitty in advance as possible — whatever happens on the day you'll still have to meet all the costs you've incurred: ground rent, donkey hire, insurance premiums, programme printing and so on. Small teams of salespeople will be more effective, as a certain amount of competition builds up between them.

The sales mathematics are simple but pretty impressive:

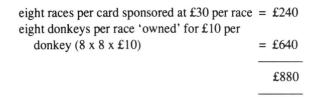

eight races per card sponsored at £30 per race = £240
eight donkeys per race 'owned' for £10 per
   donkey (8 x 8 x £10)   = £640
                                    £880

Add to this the advertising revenue and advance programme sales based on at least 50 pence per programme (to include admission), and you can see that you could be into profit before a single bet is placed on the day.

4.   When all the sponsorship, 'ownership' and advertising space are sold, get your programmes printed and start selling them. Number the programmes and offer a Lucky Programme Draw to take place at the event. This will promote programme sales, encouraging people to turn out, and you don't need expensive prizes. Maybe one or two of your sponsors would contribute these.

The rules

The rules must be prominently shown in the programme. You must also include a special notice about the tote procedure, so that you won't be liable for the Inland Revenue Totalisator Tax, which would require you to hand over 40 per cent of your tote takings to the government. There's an accepted way of getting round this. Lay out the rules, including any others that might be appropriate to your event, and the special notice thus:

RULES

1.   No jockey shall weigh more than eight stones (50 kg).
2.   No jockey may carry a whip or wear spurs or use a similar means of inducement.
3.   In the event of a rider falling off during a race, he or she may remount at the place of the fall.
4.   The judges' decision is final. Official announcements of decisions will be made through the public address system.

RACE 3

KATY'S CAKES MINI STAKES

Donkey	*Owner*
1. Currant Bun (by Instant Mix out of The Oven)	Mrs K. Jolley
2. Six Of Us	The Benson Clan
3. Dun Droppin'	Jimmy Staggers
4. My Car's Anybody's for 500 Quid	Emma Smith
5. Peaches 'n' Cream (by Tinopener out of Can Can)	Millie Crow
6. Just One Cornetto (by Pava out of Rotti)	Delicci's Delicious Ice-cream
7. Four-Legged Fiend	Jones Minimarket
8. Super Burro	Rev A.B. Oliphant

KATY'S PATISSERIE

29 The High Street
Shakybridge

FOR THE TASTIEST CAKES IN THE COUNTY

Best wishes to the Peter Pan Play Project

Figure 8. A typical page from a race-card

5. The organisers will not be responsible for any loss or damage arising from any accident or any other cause.
6. The organisers reserve the right to refuse admission to any person or animal and to expel any person or animal from the meeting without being liable for compensation.
7. Cars are parked at the owner's risk.
8. Betting will be by Totalisator Lottery.
9. Betting will be in 50 pence units.
10. The stewards and organisers cannot under any circumstances be called upon to adjudicate in any betting dispute.
11. No dogs allowed.

SPECIAL NOTICE

The Inland Revenue is obliged by Act of Parliament to deduct at source 40 per cent of all stakes invested in a Totalisator. To avoid paying this tax, and therefore giving you a much larger dividend, the Totalisator will operate as follows: Bets will be accepted up to TWO MINUTES before the start of each race. At this point an announcement will be made that betting has ceased on that event. The donkeys will then be numbered and will proceed to the start to give you an opportunity to see which animal carries your money. This procedure eliminates form and becomes pure chance and therefore not liable to the 40 per cent duty.

Officials

Identify your officials in the programme. A typical list might include:

- Starter
- Judge
- Clerk of the Course
- Tote Organiser
- Announcer/commentator
- Jockey Marshal
- Master of Donkeys
- First Aid
- Stewards
- Litter clearance

Provide every official with an easily spotted lapel badge.

Car parking

Car parking must be organised so that there's no obstruction of public roads. If parking space is limited, make this clear in your publicity. You might want to provide a VIP car park for officials, sponsors, advertisers and others who have given special support. Provide such people with lapel badges and car stickers in advance, for easy identification. This is one small way of acknowledging support and it costs very little. Make your loyal and enthusiastic supporters feel special — they are.

The tote

All betting is done by Totalisator Lottery. It simplifies things (and swells your profits) if you pay out on winning numbers only. Don't have 'place' bets. Keep the odds low, at 2:1 or 3:1. Your objective is to raise money while offering a bit of fun and mild excitement — you're not catering for serious gamblers.

The Clerk of the Course should pay out on winning tickets at the end of each race when winners present their tickets at the payout station. A different coloured ticket for each race prevents any punter dishonestly claiming a win on another race's ticket.

To avoid the Totalisator Tax all bets must be placed *before* the donkeys are numbered, so that no study of form can be made. Don't print a timetable of races, just 'Race 1, Race 2' and so on. This allows you to go on taking bets for as long as business for that race remains brisk (within reason, of course — you can't drag the proceedings out too much). When you judge the time to be right, announce on the public address system that betting on that race has now closed. The donkeys are then numbered at random and the jockeys mount according to their numbered cards (see below). Then 'They're off', after the required two minutes.

Jockeys

You need young jockeys with some riding experience. Donkeys can travel at considerable speed and a race is nothing like a sedate walk or trot along the beach. Invite children from a riding school or pony club to take part.

So that they all have a fair chance of a ride, have ready eight cards numbered 1-8 plus as many blanks as it takes to let everyone draw a card. The jockeys for each race are those who draw a numbered card for that race, and they mount the donkeys matching those numbers. This avoids arguments about who rides in which race or who rides which donkey.

What about prizes?

Lay out a little of your advance takings on a small plaque each for the winning jockey and the winning 'owner' in each race. This is always appreciated, as is giving every young jockey, whether a winner or not, a rosette or other token as a 'thank you' for taking part.

The course

Lay the course out in a horse-shoe shape measuring 150-200 yards (about 140-185 metres) from start to finish. This layout is best as the donkeys then start and finish near their enclosure. It's also easier for spectators, especially the smaller children, to see both the start and the finish.

The horse-shoe course also benefits your fund-raising. It encourages people to walk around it, passing the various stalls and side-shows where you hope they'll also spend money.

Although the course is usually described as being 'roped-off', you can't use actual ropes, as they're too easy to climb and tug about. The 'ropes' should be hurdles, fencing or sheep net.

Bar, VIP tent, stalls and side-shows

A bar or beer-tent is always profitable. (You'll need a licence — see under Licensing Laws in Chapter 6). You might also set up a VIP tent for those special supporters. An invitation to use such an amenity can often be the factor that clinches sales of advertising and race sponsorship.

Refreshment stalls of all kinds always do good business. You can run these yourselves or grant concessions to others in return for a flat rent or an agreed percentage of their takings.

Other popular attractions are:

- children's rides
- lucky dip
- a fortune teller
- balloons
- a bouncy castle
- candy floss
- popcorn

Offer as many amusements as you can fit in. People appreciate good value for money, whatever the cause, and you want them to support future events, too.

You'll find suppliers of most attractions in *Yellow Pages*, in the *Showman's Directory*, and the *World's Fair*. For a specialist service contact The Kite and Balloon Company, who have experience in fund-raising projects and offer several products ideally suited for this purpose. These include balloons for balloon races, balloons and helium gas sold at bulk rate for retail sale at events, balloon releases and drops, balloon art, kites (including promotional kites), bouncy castle hire and candy floss machines. The company will be happy to advise clients on how to best use their products for fund-raising. Managing Director Andrew V. Yeates will be delighted to send you further information, a catalogue and current price lists, and to discuss your specific requirements.

What facilities will you need?
You need to arrange:

● Adequate toilet facilities, if these are not already available at your site. Look in *Yellow Pages* under 'Toilets - Portable', or consult the *Showman's Directory* and *World's Fair* weekly.

● A first aid post (perhaps with a Lost Children point, too). Your local branch of **St John Ambulance** or the **British Red Cross Society** will advise you on this, and will usually be willing to man the post for you. You'll be expected to make a donation to their funds, and they'll appreciate a prominent acknowledgement in your programme. It wouldn't hurt, either, to remind the public that these bodies are constantly in need of both personnel and funds.

● A clean-up squad to remove litter and generally leave the venue in a clean and tidy state. A local youth group might undertake this for you.

Recommended reading
The *Showman's Directory*, an annual publication listing all kinds of services and suppliers of equipment, from caterers to creches, from marquees to mobile generators, from floodlights to fireworks. It also lists countrywide shows and festivals with their venues and dates.

The World's Fair, a weekly newspaper covering fairs and entertainments all over the country, and carrying advertisements for related services, goods and equipment. Publishes news about events, showpeople and their concerns.

CAR BOOT SALES

You can raise money from car boot sales in two ways, either renting a pitch at someone else's sale or running a sale of your own.

How do we rent a pitch?
You book your pitch in advance, gather your stock, arrive on the day and park your car or van in a designated spot. You'll need two or three helpers (or teams of helpers working in relays) and as much stock as you can load

into your vehicle. You can sell just about anything here — anything legal, that is: books and magazines, unwanted clothing and household items, crockery, toys, any old bits and pieces . . . You need:

● A table to display your stock (but check this — some authorities insist that goods be sold direct from the car boot); a folding card table or pasting table is ideal, and if you won't be needing it again you can sell it off, too, when stock gets low.

● Boxes to hold books, records, T-shirts, shoes and so on.

● A poster or banner to let people know that yours is a charity stall. You could also have leaflets and brochures handy so you don't have to spend selling time explaining who you are (but always make time to talk to potential supporters). You also need to keep your attention focused on your stall rather than allowing yourself to be engaged in conversation while the enquirer's accomplice helps himself to your stock. That's not a casual or particularly cynical remark — car boot sales attract their share of petty thieves. Keep small, easily pocketable items well back from the front of the table. You could also hand out leaflets advertising your up-coming events.

● At least two people on duty at all times, both for security and to make sure nobody gets tired of waiting to be served.

● A cash float, with plenty of small change. Prices are generally pretty low, with many items selling for less than £1. You might want to keep a supply of change hidden in a secure place inside your vehicle (which you shouldn't leave unattended for a second). Don't keep either your takings or your change in a box on the table or even on a chair behind it. Provide your helpers with strong money satchels, if they don't already have them. Sturdy bum-bags are fine. What you need is something that can be worn on the body, for maximum security.

Outlay
Charges for a pitch vary upwards from £5 for a car and £8 for a van, prepaid. To go in on the day without prior booking could mean paying anything from £1 up per pitch as a surcharge. Some organisers might be prepared to reduce the rent or even waive it altogether for a charitable cause, especially if they expect to have a few pitches to spare. It's always worth asking. However, unless the organiser is specially sympathetic to

your cause, don't expect any concessions if it's a popular sale with a waiting list for places.

Could we run our own sale?

Car boot sales are not difficult to organise and run, provided you do the groundwork thoroughly. Look for a site in the most advantageous position possible. Ideally, this would be near a busy shopping centre on the fringe of a fairly affluent residential area, and within easy walking distance of a densely populated but less well off district. This would give you the best of all situations, of course, where your event would be easily accessible to a wide diversity of customers. You'll probably have to settle for a compromise site.

Check with the police and with the local authority about permits, insurance liabilities, safety factors and so on. You'll be responsible for seeing that the sale is properly stewarded, that cars and vans enter and leave the ground in an orderly way, and that there are no traffic or pedestrian obstructions.

Members of your group and sympathetic friends might want to take an active part, collecting goods and selling them on your behalf, and some might want to help on the basis of giving you a percentage of their takings. It's up to you to decide whether you'll allow the latter a rent-free or rent-reduced pitch.

Make sure there are toilet facilities available nearby.

Publicity

Advertise the sale at least two or three weeks ahead, with a follow-up advertisement the week of the event. You can usually negotiate a discount on advertising if you book a short series rather than a one-off, and some publications offer reduced rates to charities. Give a contact phone number for bookings. If you can't man the phone constantly, you should state the hours when calls can be taken. Don't forget to check with the owners of the site how many vehicles can be accommodated, and make sure you don't overbook — you'll be very unpopular if you do. Put posters up at least a week before the sale, and provide car stickers for anyone willing to display them.

Should we charge an entrance fee?

This needs some thought. The obvious advantage is that you might take a substantial amount of money on the gate. Bear in mind, however, that charging the public to come in might impose certain responsibilities about licences and insurance cover. Check this with your local authority.

Entrance fees also mean that you have to man all the entrances at all times, which could strain your manpower resources, especially if there are several ways into your site.

Vendors generally prefer that the public be admitted free of charge — they feel that entrance fees discourage attendance and therefore cut their takings.

How often could we hold sales?

Car boot sales held regularly on the same site build up a steady custom. However, there could be restrictions on how often a particular site can be used for this purpose without planning permission. If you can clear it with the local authority, you might be able to take turns with other groups to run regular sales on the same site. Six groups working on a rota could each run two sales a year, which would almost guarantee a healthy regular attendance. Both vendors and customers will mark the dates in their diaries. And the publicity is self-generating, cutting advertising costs. The public will come anyway, whichever group is running the current sale.

What about commercial traders?

Be cautious about renting pitches to commercial traders. Their presence could upgrade your sale to market status, with subsequent legal and tax complications. Not only that, you could be inviting complaints from local traders who might claim that you're allowing an unfair advantage to commercial enterprises trading on your site at low rent and without overheads.

Be particularly careful about Sunday sales. Any commercial trading on your site could be contravening current Sunday trading laws, however anomalous these might be. Even if the local authority inspectors are sympathetic to your cause, and to your innocence, they might be obliged to bring an action against your organisation for permitting illegal trading. Check the local situation with the relevant authority.

Tightening up

To combat the increasing use of car boot sales as outlets for stolen or otherwise dubious goods, many local authorities are tightening up their procedures for granting licences. (It's stretching credibility a bit too far, they say, to see a 'householder' offering half a dozen television sets 'surplus to his family's requirements'.)

Stockport Council, for instance, in its leaflet *Conditions for Consent to Hold a Car Boot Sale*, cites its right and policy not to permit any markets to be held without its consent and stipulates: 'Only registered charities and Parent Teachers Associations to be eligible for consent. Consents for other non-profit making bodies are at the discretion of the Director of Administration.'

MARKET STALLS

If there's a regular market in your town (either indoors or out) you might be able to rent a stall there occasionally. See the Market Superintendent, who will tell you if this is possible and on what terms. Some markets have a policy of letting one charity or voluntary group per week have a stall rent free, others offer concessionary rates.

10
Indoor Events

A COLOURFUL EVENING

Mac Tompsett is the top consultant in the UK (and one of the top four in Europe) for **Colour Me Beautiful**. This is a system that helps build self-confidence by showing men and women how to choose the colours and styles of clothing that best suit their colouring, body lines and personality. Consultants' services range from advising on corporate image and company training to running individual or very small group studio sessions on colour in dress and make-up, and wardrobe planning and budgeting.

> 'Have you ever wondered what is the secret of being well dressed, having confidence in choosing colours and styles guaranteed to suit you — and being able to do it on a budget? So have thousands of others. It can be taught, and it's a subject that will always attract and fascinate an audience. Offer people an entertaining evening of hints and ideas for their personal image, and your fund-raising will be fun for everyone concerned as well as profitable for your cause.'
>
> Mac Tompsett

Mac speaks to charity and fund-raising organisations, banks and businesses, with audiences of 30 to 600, and over the last few years has helped organisations raise considerable funds for a variety of causes. For charity organisations she offers special speaking rates that cover her travelling and printing costs, and will help groups assess the best way of planning local events. Drawing on her wide experience, Mac offers the following advice to organisers:

1. Always make enquiries and bookings well ahead. Consultants are kept very busy, especially at peak times like the months leading up to Christmas.

2. Let the consultant know how many people are likely to attend, so she can plan copies of handouts for the audience. In some cases there might be a minimum attendance requirement.

3. Tell the consultant about the type of audience you expect — age range, mixed or single sex, students, possibly mixed language — so that an appropriate talk can be planned.

4. Discuss with the consultant what subject would best suit your audience, such as colour, style, make-up.

5. If there will be a sizeable audience, check that your local consultant is comfortable talking to a large number of people. If not, consult Colour Me Beautiful headquarters for one who will speak to larger groups.

6. Sound: if the audience numbers more than say 100, you'll need to arrange for amplification.

7. Lighting: colour consultants need good lighting. Check the lighting at the venue in advance, and if necessary arrange that the lightest area of the room is available and that the lighting can be turned up or otherwise augmented.

8. Sockets: a convenient socket point is essential if slides are to be shown. Check if a screen and projector are available, and if the projector is suitable for the slides the consultant intends to show. Make sure there is a spare bulb and check that the room can be adequately blacked out.

9. Easel/whiteboard/flipchart: check if these will be needed and if so whether they are available at the venue.

10. Tables: the consultant usually needs a large table for exhibits and a smaller one from which to speak.

11. Seating: demonstrations are very visual, so you need to make sure that everyone has a good view. If possible, arrange the seating in a semi-circular or half-horseshoe shape rather than in straight rows. If the audience will be seated round small tables, arrange for them to be asked to turn their chairs and settle themselves comfortably facing towards the speaker before the talk begins. This avoids chair-turning

and movement that could disrupt the first few minutes of the talk, and should also reduce distracting restlessness when members of the audience need to shift to more comfortable positions every few minutes.

12. Let the consultant know beforehand whether you would like some books supplied for sale purposes at the talk, or whether this is against the policy of your charity.

13. Length of talk/demonstration: this can vary from 20 to 50 minutes, depending on the subject. You need to know, so that you can allow time for questions and organise any refreshments that are to be served afterwards.

14. Cost: this depends on the consultant's experience and qualifications, and on the size of the audience. For fund-raising, Colour Me Beautiful consultants will often waive their professional rates and attend for a nominal fee to cover expenses, plus a small reimbursement for time spent away from their studios.

15. Publicity: contact the local press before the event, and if it seems appropriate send an invitation for a journalist and photographer to attend. There is no guarantee they will come, however, so make sure someone takes a few photographs (black and white is best for this purpose) so that you can send one or two with a report after the event. The consultant will supply you with a poster or handout which can be used in ticket printing and for publicity.

16. Tickets: these can help with fund-raising, as many people will buy a ticket rather than give a donation. You'll also find that people are more likely to attend the event if they are committed by ticket. This makes it easier for you to plan seating and to budget for refreshments.

17. Raffle: if your event includes a raffle, the consultant may donate a prize of a 10 per cent discount on a colour class, or, if the audience is larger, she may donate a book as a prize.

The Colour Me Beautiful books (all published by Piatkus Books) are: *Colour Me Beautiful, Colour for Men, Colour Me Beautiful Makeup Book,* all by Carole Jackson, and *The Colour Me Beautiful Complete Style Guide* by Mary Spillane.

Colour Me Beautiful consultants can help you raise funds in other ways, too:

A stall at your fair or exhibition

Check the following points with the consultant:

1. Always ask what she needs in terms of table space, back boards and so on.

2. Make sure the hours of attendance are mutually agreed and clearly understood.

3. Clarify whether you require items for sale, books for example, to be featured on the demonstration stall.

4. Advise the consultant if there will be an opportunity for a short presentation, say a ten-minute slot at a specified time, which could be featured in your advertising material and also advertised at the entrance to the venue. This could attract people to come in just to see the demonstration, and once people are inside they will usually look at whatever else is on offer — and spend money. (You would need to site the demonstration stall in a spot where people could gather round several deep without causing too much obstruction for your other attractions.)

Articles for charity magazines and newspapers

If you are producing your own magazine or newspaper, or are raising money on behalf of a charity that has a publication, Colour Me Beautiful consultants will often be willing to contribute an article or a series of articles. Discuss the subject matter with the consultant, and allow enough time for her to prepare the article(s). There are many topics that would be of interest and that could boost sales of the publication:

- colour
- style
- make-up
- how to make the best of yourself
- dressing for a wedding
- organising and planning a wardrobe
- dressing on a budget
- question and answer article

Mac suggests that you might include a small advertisement in your publication, in return for the contributed article(s).

Mac Tompsett is based in Gresford, midway between Wrexham, North Wales, and Chester, Cheshire. Full details are in the appendices.

The advice Mac Tompsett has given here could be very usefully applied to any talks or demonstrations you might arrange. Such thorough attention to detail reflects the meticulous planning needed for successful fund-raising. The check-list below will help you ensure that you haven't overlooked any vital point in organising your event.

Checklist for a talk or demonstration

		Yes	Date	Payment made
1.	Speaker(s) booked	☐	_____	_____
	confirmed in writing	☐	_____	_____
2.	Venue booked	☐	_____	_____
	confirmed in writing	☐	_____	_____
3.	Venue checked for:		_____	_____
	lighting	☐	_____	_____
	sound	☐	_____	_____
	projector	☐	_____	_____
	sockets	☐	_____	_____
	speaker's table(s)	☐	_____	_____
4.	Catering arranged		_____	_____
	confirmed in writing	☐	_____	_____
5.	Licences and insurance arranged		_____	_____
	(if applicable)	☐	_____	_____
6.	Programme printing arranged	☐	_____	_____
7.	Publicity arranged:		_____	_____
	press release/editorial	☐	_____	_____
	local radio	☐	_____	_____
	posters	☐	_____	_____
	leaflets	☐	_____	_____
8.	Photography arranged for press		_____	_____
	follow-up report	☐	_____	_____

CRAFT FAIRS

Craft fairs are held all over the country all year round. They are becoming increasingly popular, both with craftspeople seeking outlets for their work and with the public looking for quality and originality. If you have people skilled in craft work of any kind among your group and its supporters, you might consider selling their work at a fair. You need to set about this in the right way, though.

How should we go about it?
Jean M. Harris has been organising fairs for over a dozen years, including antiques, collectors' and arts and crafts fairs, although her main interest is in craft fairs. Jean advises that it would not be a viable fund-raising enterprise to try to run a 'one-off' craft fair yourselves. The costs involved are very high, because the organiser is responsible for hiring the venue, the tables, electrical equipment, special lighting, as well as arranging printing and advertising, insurances and so on. To be sure of covering these expenses and making a profit, you would have to charge vendors a very high stall rent. And if the event turned out to be a financial flop, you could find your group in debt instead of in profit. Jean makes the emphatic point that professional craftspeople are very wary of 'amateur' organisers, and you would find it difficult to attract the standard of exhibitors needed to ensure a successful fair.

Selling at an established fair
It would be far better, Jean says, for your group to sell craft goods at an established fair, where the high standard and good reputation of the organiser almost guarantee a good attendance of both exhibitors and public. Your financial risks would then be limited to the cost of hiring a stall, and the worst that could happen is that you might not sell enough to cover that. At a well attended and well organised fair, however, that isn't likely to happen.

Stall-hire charges at Jean's fairs range from around £16 up to £28 a day for a six-foot-long stall, rising according to the size of stall and the date and location. Jean operates a 'free admission' policy which ensures a good attendance — an essential factor, she says, in attracting and satisfying her craftspeople clients.

Jean suggests that before you book with any organiser, you go along to at least one of their fairs to see how well it has been organised. Regrettably, there are some very bad organisers around. You can learn a lot about any event from initial impressions, and from a general assessment of the organisation and the quality of the goods on display. Check, too, how well the fair has been promoted, because without good promotion a fair is unlikely to attract a large enough public attendance to make your participation worthwhile.

A good organiser will check the quality of craftspeople's products, asking to see actual samples before renting space to them. If the goods you see on display when you check out a fair are of a mediocre standard, regard it as a warning sign that the organiser's standards are none too high either. You won't do your cause much good if you find yourself, however unwittingly, trying to sell quality goods at an event that would be more honestly described as a flea market.

'Whatever you do, have a professional approach to it and have plenty of stock to sell, as there is nothing worse than running out of stock when customers are eager to buy from you.'

Jean M. Harris

What to sell

The type of goods you'll sell will depend on the specific skills of those supporters willing to contribute to the enterprise. The goods you sell should be attractive, very well made, and hand-crafted for preference. Remember that a good fair organiser (and you won't be dealing with any other kind, if you're wise) will expect your stock to be up to the standard of the other exhibitors, and you should be prepared to have samples examined before your booking is accepted. However willing he or she might be to help your cause, the organiser can't afford to alienate regular exhibitors by giving space to goods that would lower the fair's overall standards.

You might have to use a bit of tact and diplomacy to avoid hurt feelings should any supporter offer you 'craftwork' that you know would not be up to the required standard for this particular event. Accept all donated items gratefully — but be selective about what finds it way on to your craft stall. Unsuitable items can be diverted to a more suitable occasion.

Recommended reading

If you need a bit of inspiration, and maybe instruction, look at some of the many excellent books that are currently available. There are books in the shops and libraries about every imaginable craft. The following books are particularly good for the types of crafts that sell well at fairs:

The Rag Doll Handbook by Ana Lakeland. Sold in some of the world's most exclusive toyshops, Ana Lakeland's rag dolls are surprisingly simple to make, and only require the most basic sewing skills. The book gives detailed patterns for the basic doll and for a really imaginative selection of variations including Snow White and the Seven Dwarfs, Santa Claus, sailors, clowns and punks, and many more. Included are instructions for making a box which could be used to display the dolls, or sold with them as gift boxes.

Making Silk Flowers by Anne Hamilton and Kathleen White. This is a book to make crafty fingers itch to get to work. With over 60 templates for flowers and foliage, it's packed with meticulously detailed instructions and lavish colour photographs of every stage of making every item. From simple sprays to wedding flowers, from Christmas wreaths to lunch arrangements, these beautiful creations would be sure sellers on your stall.

Easy to Make Knitted Toys by Joy Gammon. Easy to follow instructions and imaginative designs for a variety of colourful soft toys that can be made very economically — the smallest needs only two or three metres of yarn. The range includes knitted dolls, cars, animals and birds, and there's even a knitted Noah's Ark complete with 'livestock'.

Easy to Patchwork by Lynette Mostaghimi. Easy to follow instructions with full colour illustrations for patchwork items including 'Suffolk puff' cushion covers, ribbon greeting cards, scented sachets, toys, clothing, even patchwork ear-rings.

The *Family Circle* series is wonderful value for money, and includes *Family Circle Best Selling Food and Craft*, which has a section on 'Craft Stall Creations', with instructions for making items like hairbands, bangles and combs, padded coat-hangers, toiletry bags, shower caps, place-mats and stencilled items.

Family Circle Beautiful Things to Make for Baby is packed with bright and interesting clothes, toys and pictures, and comes complete with a large sheet of trace-off patterns.

Family Circle Kids' Knits and Crochet has fun-to-wear clothes for the fashion-conscious pre-teens — and some patterns for huggable toys, as a bonus.

Family Circle Soft Toys to Sew has instructions for making a wonderfully imaginative selection of very desirable soft toys. The children will love Hortense the Hippo, Leonard the Lion, Spike the Fire-breathing Dragon, Teddies in Vests and Bunnies in Bows.

A variety or a theme?

What you can offer will depend, of course, on what stock you can gather, but if you think your stall would be most successful if you stick to a limited number of types of goods, you should let prospective contributors know what kind of items you require well in advance of the date.

For instance, if your cause is connected with children, you might think it appropriate to limit your display to toys and/or children's clothing. Around Christmas, you could offer a selection of small Christmas gifts and stocking fillers. You should aim to make your display as attractive as possible, and it's easier to do this if you work to a theme rather than have an uncoordinated mix of items.

Sales techniques

It's worth having a word with those who will be manning your stall, especially if they have little or no previous experience of selling at fairs. They need to understand that pushy selling can be counter-productive. People come to craft fairs to *look* at beautiful and interesting things, and don't expect to rush in, buy the first thing that attracts them, then leave. They like to browse at their leisure, to assess values, to take time over their decisions. It's all part of their enjoyment. For the most part, browsers find it very off-putting to be 'collared' by over-enthusiastic vendors. You probably know the type. They leap to their feet the instant you pause in front of their stall, and launch into sales talk, even thrusting items under the poor customer's nose in their eagerness to point out the merits of their work. Whether this is done from genuine enthusiasm about their craft or whether they are over-eager to clinch a sale, the result is usually the same: the customer will be uneasy, maybe even resentful of the pressure, and will almost invariably edge away as soon as is politely possible, or even sooner.

It's much more effective simply to smile and nod acknowledgement of the customer's presence, so that they know you've noticed them and are available should they want to buy or even to ask about your goods. Leave them in peace to browse, to examine, to compare, to be tempted, maybe to wander off and then come back. . . you'll find that as often as not they'll talk themselves into buying. They'll enjoy the whole process, won't feel they've been forced into any kind of corner, and so won't feel the need to avoid your stall next time round. Don't forget that you're in the business of building goodwill as well as making money.

It's polite to ask

Check with the organiser before you put any brochures or collecting boxes on display on your stall. The organiser might have reasons for not wanting this, and even if you believe there would be no objections, it's polite to ask.

Finding the fairs

Organisers who are active in your area will usually advertise in the local papers. These advertisements, however, are aimed at attracting the public, so will appear too late for you to book. You need to know well in advance when and where a suitable fair will be held. You can find this out by contacting local organisers and asking for a list of future dates.

You can also consult *The Craftsman* magazine, where advance time-tables are printed regularly, and where many organisers advertise. The magazine *Popular Crafts* also lists some forthcoming fairs, but its coverage is not so comprehensive as that of *The Craftsman.*

BOOK FAIRS

In the section on craft fairs you're advised to take a stall at someone else's event rather than attempt to run your own. The reverse applies to book fairs. For a start, you'd probably find it very difficult to persuade an organiser to give you space; there's almost invariably a waiting list of professional dealers hoping for a place at established events. Many dealers earn a large part of their living at fairs, where they trade with each other as well as with the public, and they'd be very unhappy with any organiser who denied them a place in favour of a 'casual', however charitable the cause.

If you're considering a book fair, then, it's best to run your own. Here's the procedure as outlined by Jill Trenholme, who has been running fairs for professional book dealers in Cheshire for over ten years. Jill emphasises the importance of preparation and groundwork. She quotes a maxim that should be every fund-raiser's watchword: 'Fail to prepare — prepare to fail'. And preparation starts six to nine months ahead.

Preparation

The date
For the benefit of exhibitors, the public and your cause, avoid clashing with any major professional fair in the region. You want to attract as many dealers as you can either to rent your stalls or to come along to buy stock, and you want the public to attend *your* fair, not someone else's. Upcoming fairs are advertised in the monthly *Book and Magazine Collector*, and listed in *Antiquarian Book Monthly Review.* You can also contact the **Provincial Booksellers Fairs Association** (PBFA), who issue a calendar of book fairs to their members, one of whom might be based in your area.

Try to organise your fair so that it complements rather than competes with the dealers' interests. This is especially important if you plan to run book fairs on any kind of regular basis. The cooperation of local dealers in particular could be invaluable.

The venue
Choose this carefully. It might be a village hall, a community centre, a hotel. . . but it must have:

- good parking and easy access for unloading and loading, with as few steps as possible — books are heavy;
- enough space for setting up an adequate number of display tables without crowding;
- a separate room for rest and refreshments, not too close to the book room, so there's no risk of spilled drinks or sticky fingers damaging books. Buyers and dealers are browsers, and like somewhere to sit and think before purchasing;
- good lighting — absolutely essential.

Costing
How many six-foot tables will your venue hold comfortably? Ask the venue manager or measure up for yourselves. Some dealers prefer to bring their own folding bookshelves rather than use a table, but six feet is the usual width allocated whether tables are used or not. You need to price your stalls so that their rents cover all your basic costs and show some profit, but the charge has to be appropriate to the venue: £10 at the most for a village hall, up to £20 for a well publicised fair at a large hotel. Remember to take into account that you'll need at least one stall for your own donated stock.

Set the entrance fee at 40 or 50 pence, with reductions for children and senior citizens.

Publicity
Ask your local paper and local radio to help. Put up posters in shop windows (especially in book shops) and in *legal* public places — take your local authority's advice on this. Car stickers, leaflets. . . everything helps. If you can find a celebrity to open your fair, high-profile publicity will be much easier to get, and the public will be keener to attend. A writer or journalist would be appropriate here, but in fact pretty well any famous person can boost your attendance figures. (See under 'Celebrity Attractions' in Chapter 7.) Entrance fees from the public will make up a substantial part of your eventual profit, so don't skimp on publicity.

You also need to publicise your fair to the dealers you hope to attract. As early as possible, have simple leaflets printed with the essential information about your fair. Compile a list of upcoming fairs in your region, and plan to go to as many as possible. Contact the organisers in advance, and ask if they'll let you distribute your leaflets to the dealers at their fairs, and if possible to the customers too. Make sure you include a contact name, address and phone number on the leaflet, for taking advance stall bookings. You can also find dealers listed in *Yellow Pages*, and many advertise in the 'Books for sale and wanted' sections in *Book and Magazine Collector*. Contact these dealers, too.

On the day

If you've declared your opening time to be, say, 10am, open the venue to exhibitors at 8am. They need time to set up, and like to trade among themselves before the public arrives. Do as much as you can to prevent 'outside' dealers getting into the hall before you let the public in — this can cause ill feeling. Issue exhibitors' badges or labels to those entitled to be there.

Layout

Allow plenty of space for people to move around, to browse and to read in comfort. If there's room, a few chairs in the book room would be welcome — browsing and buying can be tiring. Limit the space you allow each dealer. See that they keep to their allocated area, and don't spread out or load on too much stock. Dealers bring their own folding bookshelves to mount on the tables, and some can't resist the temptation to bring their entire stock of books. Overloaded shelves or boxes that jut out can be a serious hazard.

Try to ensure that there's a good variety of stalls — you don't want a hall full of paperbacks or children's annuals.

Opening time

Open the doors to the public on the dot of the time advertised. Issue a ticket as each customer pays. People will want to come and go between the book room, refreshment area, toilets, car park and so on, and they should keep their tickets for readmission. Make sure you have an adequate cash float.

Some tips from Jill:

1. Your own stall: before the event, offer a local dealer first look in return for advice on pricing (and in case someone has given you a valuable item). You'll have to keep the prices of your own stock fairly low, as it will probably all have been donated and everybody will know you'll be making 100 per cent profit on it.

2.   Make it a rule that stall rents are paid 'up front' at the time of booking, so that you won't lose financially through any dealer's non-appearance.

3.   Encourage interesting displays by offering a prize for the best display given the limited space. Books can look a bit dull, and imaginative displays add interest to the whole event.

4.   Provide paper bags for wrapping books as they're sold. This helps to discourage the lightfingered (and there are always a few of those around) by identifying paid-for purchases. Perhaps a local company would donate a supply of bags with their name or logo on them, in return for the publicity this gives.

5.   A local youth group might be willing to help with unloading in the morning, and loading and clearing up after the event.

THEME PARTIES

You can organise a party on any theme, and make it as simple or as lavish as you like. People will respond to something that's a little different.

● a Tudor feast is fun, with punch or mead to drink, chops and chicken legs to gnaw, and a minstrel or bard to entertain;
● a nursery tea lets the juvenile in every adult tuck into sausage and mash, jelly and custard;
● a Wild West party or a hoe-down, with fiddles and square-dancing, gives everyone a chance to let their hair down, especially if you can find a barn to hold it in.

Barbecue food is a good choice for something like the last event — there's nothing like a bit of smoke for an 'open-air' flavour — and Carole Handslip's book *Barbecues* (Merehurst) is a very reasonably priced treasury of barbecue recipes: Spanish chorizo sausages, chicken tikka, fillet steak on garlic toast, spit-roast lamb, Turkish kebabs — there's plenty here for the most seasoned barbecue fan.

Parties for all nations
On a more gastronomic theme, try a 'national' party. For example, for an Italian party you could transform a room, hall or garden into 'Old Napoli'

using red, white and green bunting and balloons (contact the Kite & Balloon Company for supplies). The food can be as cheap and cheerful or as exotic as you want. Armed with a copy of Evelyne Slomon's *The Pizza Book*, you'll not only surprise your guests with an astonishing variety of pizzas, you'll impress them, too, with your knowledge of the pizza's origins and history. Why not prepare enough extra pizzas — many of the recipes are for pizzas that are equally good hot or cold — and sell or auction them while people are still excited by what they're eating. Romantic Italian music could help to induce generosity.

Alternatively, you could throw a more sophisticated Italian party and delight your guests with some of the *Festive Food of Italy* featured in Maddalena Bonino's book, published by Kyle Cathie. These are traditional recipes marking saints' days, feast days and festivals all over Italy (with fascinating information about the occasions). Who could resist Torta Pasqualine (Easter Pie) or Fiore di Mandorlo (almond biscuits for the Feast of the Flowering Almond Tree). Well entertained and well fed guests respond most favourably to fund-raising appeals.

In the same series, Kyle Cathie also publish *The Festive Food of America, China, Spain, England* and *France*, so you've plenty of variety in themes to choose from.

Cultural contacts

Most countries have a cultural presence in our big cities. It's worth contacting their UK representatives — embassies, consulates and so on — to ask if they could send along a speaker to talk about their culture and traditions, and perhaps arrange for entertainers to attend your function.

SALES PARTIES

Jewellery, lingerie, leisure-wear, cosmetics, greeting cards, kitchen-ware . . . Sales parties are proving ever more popular as fund-raisers. They're easy to organise, as they're usually held in private homes and catered for in much the same way as private parties. Attendance is by invitation, so the numbers can be as few or as many as you like.

Like coffee mornings, these parties can either be run to raise a one-off donation to the cause or to help fund a larger event.

There are many party-plan agents around the country selling on behalf of national and international companies whose products are standardised — you'll see the same range in Exeter, Eccles or Edinburgh. However, if you take time to ask around and investigate in your locality, you'll probably find that there are others who offer more original and interesting products like hand-crafted goods, natural cosmetics, hand-made toys and so on. Often these are craftspeople who offer their own products and those of other local people working in the same line. Standards are usually pretty high, as the success of these businesses depends on building and maintaining a good reputation.

Before you commit yourself to anything, though, always ask to see the products — you can't afford to trust to luck as far as quality is concerned.

A jewellery party

One example of such an event is a jewellery party, like those at which Carol Fielding operates her business 'Touch of Class'. Carol travels anywhere within a 40-mile radius of her base in Accrington, Lancashire. She says that besides raising useful funds, she finds that the parties she attends give a welcome opportunity for hard-working fund-raisers to give themselves a respite from organising other events.

> I always find that the ladies really enjoy this kind of event. By having the party separate from an event where there are lots of activities and stalls, those who are involved in running the larger events are able to relax and enjoy themselves with friends.
>
> Carol Fielding

Morning, afternoon or evening events are all popular. The hostess sends out invitation cards (which Carol has available) about two weeks prior to the party, perhaps following up with a reminder a day or two before the date. You can make a charge for attendance, if you wish, to cover the cost of simple refreshments and perhaps add a little to the overall profits too. Provide tea, coffee, soft drinks, possibly wine which is easy to serve and adds to the party atmosphere.

The party
On the day, Carol arrives at the venue about one hour before the starting time, to set up her jewellery. Most of her stock is hand-crafted and exclusive. For your own party, look for someone who, like Carol, can offer a range which appeals to all ages and tastes, from classical pearls and Austrian crystal, cloisonné, hand-crafted leather, copper-covered leaves, to 'magic' colour-change jewellery, pens and children's brooches, and an original range of hand-crafted mirrors.

This is more than just a sales party, though. Carol also gives a talk about the different types of jewellery and about the individuals who make them, spicing her talk with amusing anecdotes and incidents. A good party sales-person will make your party a truly enjoyable event.

This combination of quality, variety and entertainment promotes sales — and sales mean commission. Carol pays a commission of 10 per cent cash or 15 per cent in goods. 'It's worth bearing in mind,' she says, 'that goods taken in commission can be raffled to raise even more money.'

One party leads to another

One of the exciting things about sales parties, as far as fund-raising is concerned, is that more often than not they result in bookings being made for future parties by people who have enjoyed the event so much that they want to hold a party of their own. This snowball effect helps to spread the word about your cause as well as raising more funds.

JUMBLE SALES

The growing popularity of car boot sales in recent years has tended to overshadow that old favourite the jumble sale. Don't write it off, though. A jumble sale is cheap and relatively easy to organise, and it can be very profitable.

Basically you need a hall, plenty of helpers and plenty of jumble. Allow plenty of time, too, to gather your jumble. Distribute leaflets to as many houses as possible, asking for donations of unwanted goods. Give a contact name and number for collection to be arranged, and if possible an address where goods can be delivered by householders willing to do so. State when and where the sale will be held, and make it clear if there are any types of goods you don't want, like bulky furniture or gas and electrical equipment.

Saturday is the most popular day, so book early, and try to avoid clashing with major events or bank holidays. Advertise your sale in the local press and local radio, in 'hand-out' leaflets and on posters. Keep your message simple and clear, making sure you include essential information:

JUMBLE SALE

SATURDAY 20TH OCTOBER
10AM

SUNNYSIDE COMMUNITY CENTRE
POND LANE, SHAKYBRIDGE
Admission 10 pence

In aid of THE PETER PAN PLAY PROJECT

Sort out the jumble before you take it to the hall. 'Jumble' doesn't mean 'rubbish', so throw away anything in really bad condition. Set a minimum (and perhaps a maximum) price for each stall, and it helps if those manning the stall can agree on a rough pricing policy before they start selling.

If your hall has the facilities, you can boost your profits with a refreshment stall.

Don't forget to arrange for the disposal of unsold jumble, and to clear up the hall afterwards.

For the know-how on running a brilliantly successful jumble sale, read *The Jumble Sale Handbook* by Frances Pitt, 'An In-Depth Exposé from Both Sides of the Trestle'. You'll find everything you could possibly need or want to know about jumble sales in this practical and informative guide (which manages to be very readable and amusing, too). It's all here: planning, preparation, publicity, managing the day, with plenty of 'insider' tips for success.

SOME IDEAS FOR YOUR CHRISTMAS FAIR

An average size community centre or church hall should accommodate enough stalls to give a good selection of attractions. When choosing your stalls, give some thought to the spending power in the neighbourhood. Where there isn't likely to be much spare money about, have plenty of goods and prizes that would make attractive Christmas presents, particularly for children, and that allow children themselves scope to spend pocketmoney. In more affluent areas you can cater for potentially bigger spenders. Offer 'collectables', quality hand-knits, costume jewellery, luxury craft items. Make sure, though, that there are plenty of bargains around as well — 'affluent' doesn't necessarily mean 'extravagant'. People with money often have it because they are careful shoppers.

The suggestions offered here are all proven money-spinners. You'll probably think of others specially suitable for your own event.

Cake stall

This is one stall where you'll never be left with unsold goods. Scones, biscuits and small cakes are always fast sellers, especially with customers who live alone. They appreciate being able to buy a few selected items rather than having to buy whole packs. A display of small cakes looks particularly tempting. Aim for a selection to suit all tastes — plain or iced sponge cakes, jam tarts, meringues, chocolate chip cookies... *Family Circle Best Selling Food and Craft* has a section on 'Cake Stall Delights' ranging from basic butter cake with flavour variations to a gingerbread family complete with dog and cat. *Miniature Novelty Cakes,* published by Merehurst, has recipes and instructions for an irresistible range in colourful miniature (about three inches) of such delights as a baby in a pink cradle, a fireworks party, a straw hat with flowers, a bride's cake and many more. You'll need plenty of stock under the counter for topping up your stall.

Family size sponges and fruit cakes sell well, too. (Don't forget to flag clearly anything that has been previously frozen.) Have some of the larger cakes available for slicing, so that you can offer individual portions.

For a really eye-catching centrepiece, feature a special Christmas cake, and if you can organise the production, have a selection of festive cakes for sale. *Sugarpaste Christmas Cakes,* also published by Merehurst, is packed with original and unusual designs, such as Father Christmas in a chimney, a Christmas pudding, a snowman, a sack of toys. There are full instructions, including templates.

For easy handling, place larger cakes on cardboard plates before you display them. Put up a prominent notice or two asking customers not to touch the food but to let your helpers pack it for them. Cake slices and tongs must be used when packing food, and take special care that no one handles both food and money.

Packing points
You need plenty of crisp, clean paper bags. This is not the place for second-hand packaging — you want your customers to feel that you value them enough to take some trouble over packing their purchases hygienically. Cardboard boxes — the kind you fold up from flat on the spot, are useful for protecting cakes. Supplies of packaging materials can be bought quite cheaply from a cash and carry, from catering specialists, and from Craft Creations.

Prehistoric delights
How do you think the children would respond to a display of *Dinosaur Cakes?* Try them with some of the fantastic recipes and designs in Jacqui Hine's book of that name, from Merehurst. Our old favourite Tyrannosaurus Rex is here, along with Brachyosaurus, Brontosaurus, Stegosaurus, and some 16 other relatives, including a colourful Dinosaur Tableau. Nobody will walk past your stall when they spot this lot.

Then there's Carole Handslip's exciting collection of *Children's Party Cakes,* 50 recipes to satisfy every child's idea of what a cake should be. There's a Big Red Bus, a Teddy Bear, a Fairy Castle, a Space Ship, a Treasure Island. You'll have plenty of satisfied customers with these.

Candy bar

The irresistible sweet stall, specially popular in the run-up to Christmas when people are on the lookout for stocking fillers and tree decorations.

Buy sweets in wholesale packs and repack them in affordable quantities. Pack some in plain plastic food bags to sell cheaply (but still at a profit), and arrange others in more elaborate packaging as gifts and decorations. The most popular quantities are 4oz (about 100g) and 8oz (225g).

Home-made fudge, peppermint creams, coconut ice — these can all be placed in paper cases and arranged in pretty boxes covered with Cellophane wrapping, which looks far more attractive than wrinkly cling-film. (Cling-film is not now recommended for any form of packaging where it comes in contact with certain foods, particularly foods with a high fat content, like fudge.) With a festive ribbon tied round them, boxes of sweets make ideal small gifts. You could also prepack some of the fudge and other home-made goodies in plastic bags — there will be plenty of people who'll want to eat them on the spot. (You'll find recipes for these best-sellers in the appendices.)

Make **tree ornaments** by cutting squares or circles of dressmaker's net, placing a few wrapped sweets in the middle and tying them up with stretchy glitter string, which is easier to manage and more secure than slippery ribbon.

Try contacting confectionery companies to ask if they have any lines they are keen to promote. Offer to mount a display and sell samples at promotion prices. Even if they don't take up this suggestion, they might donate some of their products. (You'll almost always stand a better chance of getting something if you offer something in return, rather than just asking for 'freebies'.)

Family Circle Best Selling Food and Craft has a mouthwatering selection of Sweet Stall Temptations, delicious recipes with some very useful Cook's Tips to help you produce the kind of stock that sells out fast.

White elephant

This doesn't cost a penny to stock, and always makes money. Household items and bric-a-brac of every imaginable kind are snapped up by eager bargain-hunters. This is where Mrs Brown falls for the purple cushion that clashed with Mrs Green's new pastel decor, and where Mr Jones pounces on a replacement of the Beatles LP his grandson used as a stand-in for his toy cars' Brand's Hatch. Pitch the prices a little higher than you'd expect to get. You might get the full price, but if a customer wants to haggle, you've left scope for that — you'll get the money and he'll get the satisfaction of having beaten you down. You'll make unbelievable amounts of money from things you wouldn't think anyone would give house-room to. The white elephant is a cliché come true — one man's junk really is another man's treasure.

If there's stock left with only half an hour to go, have an announcement made that everything on the stall is now half-price (or even 5 pence an item, if nobody is willing to store the left-over stuff).

Note: electrical goods
It's against the law to offer electrical appliances with the now defunct red, green and black wiring, other than as collectors' items or ornaments, in which case you should cut off the wires as close to the item's body as possible. Don't offer any modern electrical goods — that is those with the brown live wire, green and yellow earth wire and blue neutral wire — without first having them thoroughly checked by a qualified electrician. Always make it clear to the purchaser that the item is second-hand and you can't guarantee it in any way. Unless you envisage getting a high price for the item, it might be best not to accept it in the first place. The price you can reasonably ask might not justify the time, trouble and expense of having it checked.

Santa's grotto
A well publicised visit from Santa is always an attraction. You need a small room or a corner of your hall that can be screened off. Try to site the grotto where a queue won't obstruct other stalls.

You also need a genial Santa, ideally one blessed with an extraordinary amount of tact and patience. Dress up the grotto with tinsel and balloons, and equip Santa with a sack of small presents. It's best to keep these presents to a uniform value, to avert accusations of favouritism (which are just as likely to come from parents as from children). You can buy suitable small toys and games from your cash and carry warehouse or from mail order specialists like Peeks of Bournemouth or Baker Ross — all these sources will supply bulk packs. Set your charge per visit according to the spending power of your expected customers. (Bulk-bought small toys cost approximately 9 to 15 pence each, so you could make a very nice profit at 25 pence per child per visit, which should be affordable even where a family has several children.)

Smile please!
If one of your volunteers has a reliable Polaroid camera, you could do a

sideline in souvenir photographs of Santa with each child. You would have to cost this carefully, as instant film is expensive. Make it clear what the charge per visit will be, with and without a photograph. (A local camera shop might let you have film at a discount, and might even lend you a demonstration camera in return for appropriate publicity.)

Toys

Second-hand toys
Be ruthless — discard anything dirty or badly worn, broken or chipped. (You could offer damaged wooden or metal toys in a bargain box beside or under your stall, making sure the box is clearly labelled 'Damaged Goods'. Someone who enjoys making or repairing toys might find spare parts there.)

Repair any fabric splits, loose eyes and so on, and make sure there are no sharp edges or points. Check that any jigsaw puzzles are complete, and pack the pieces in a plastic bag inside the box so that none can be lost if someone opens the box.

Look out for possible collectors' items. Old toys from makers like Dinky and Hornby can be valuable, especially if they come with their original boxes. Take such items to a specialist dealer, or save them for a collectors' fair.

New toys
Offer a varied choice, with something for all ages. Baker Ross can supply a range of small, fun toys costing from a few pence upwards, as do many cash-and-carry outlets.

If there's a toy manufacturer in your area, they might be willing to donate a few toys — it's always worth asking.

Soft toys
These are always good sellers. There are many pattern books in the shops and libraries, and 'family' magazines often carry features and pull-out supplements devoted to fund-raising makes. Among the best are *Family Circle, Woman's Weekly, Woman's Realm, Woman and Home, Prima* and *Essentials.* Look for simple yet colourful patterns. Ana Lakeland's *The Rag Doll Handbook* and Joy Gammon's *Easy to Make Knitted Toys* can help you here, as can *Family Circle Soft Toys to Sew* (see under Craft Fairs).

Dolls of all kinds are always popular, from the traditional 'baby' doll to the glamorous Sindy-type fashion doll. Both types are available without clothes from your cash-and-carry, or from one of the suppliers who advertise in the craft magazines. You can dress these dolls for very little money, from remnants of fabric and scraps of lace and ribbons, and sell them very profitably at prices far lower than those charged in the shops.

Kiddies' corner

If there's room, set aside a corner well away from the entrance, where parents can leave their children for a few minutes under responsible supervision. You can make a small charge for this, or provide the service as an amenity so that parents can browse around your fair by themselves.

Provide a low table, mats, a few toys and games, books, Lego, dressing-up clothes.

Make sure the children are under constant surveillance. You might also want to operate some kind of security system, perhaps giving a 'receipt' to be handed over when the child is collected. Make it clear that there is a time limit — say half an hour — on the facility. Your aim is to make it easy for the parents to spend money at your event — you're not offering a free afternoon's child-minding.

11
More Fund-Raising Ideas

TELEVISION AND RADIO APPEALS

Every year we marvel as millions of pounds pour into marathon fund-raising events like *Children in Need*, *Telethon* and *Comic Relief*. And every year the totals get bigger and bigger as the public digs ever deeper into its collective pocket. Your cause might be able to get a share.

National media fund-raising events get lots of advance publicity. As soon as you see the first signs, ring up the appropriate TV and radio stations and ask if your cause might be eligible to receive some of the money raised. You might get an outright 'thumbs-down' if your cause is not considered suitable for an allocation from that particular event, but better a quick 'No' now than a lot of time wasted writing an application that would have been binned anyway. If there is even a faint chance, ask for an application form.

Diana Leat's book *Fundraising and Grant Making: A Case Study of ITV Telethon '88* analyses the organisation of the first Telethon, how the money was raised, how it was spent, the dilemmas involved in assessing 22,000 applications. It also looks at the relationship between charity, Telethon and the state. It makes very informative reading.

In comparison with national TV appeals, radio appeals raise quite small amounts of money. However, if your cause is one that is likely to touch hearts and minds beyond your locality, it might be worth trying for a spot on *The Week's Good Cause*, the regular appeal on BBC Radio 4. Contact the programme producer at the BBC (his or her name usually appears in *Radio Times*, and is credited at the end of the programme) and present your case as persuasively as you can.

Local radio

Local radio is probably your best bet. Although an appeal on local radio, whether BBC or independent, won't reach as large an audience as a national appeal, the people it does reach are more likely to respond to a local cause.

Make contact with the managers of your local BBC and independent stations, to see if they can help either directly with appeals for gifts and donations or indirectly by publicising your events. You might be able to get a spot to make your own appeal. (See the Publicity section in Chapter 3.)

It would be useful to read *Broadcast Charitable Appeals: The Opportunities for Getting Support from Local Radio*, by Diana Leat; this is a study of the contribution of local radio to charitable appeals.

CHRISTMAS CARDS

Christmas cards are big business for many national charities. Your organisation might be too local to take part in the schemes run by the **Charity Christmas Card Council** (4C) which are only open to national and international charities, but you might find it useful to enquire about criteria for membership and to see their Christmas Card Directory which lists the charities who are members — your organisation could grow in the future.

Even if you don't want to go into the Christmas card market in anything like a big way, you'll find the **Charities Advisory Trust** book *Charity Christmas Cards: How to Produce Them, How to Sell Them, How to Make Money from Them*, by Hilary Blume, very informative.

Most people like to buy some charity cards each Christmas, but many say they would buy more if the designs were better. Perhaps your group could produce a card, or a small range of cards, that would be attractive and economical enough to sell locally, promoting your cause while adding to your funds.

How do we make it appealing?
You need a good design. This could be an original drawing, photograph or painting, either produced by a group member or supporter or commissioned from a professional, depending on the economics involved. You don't want to pay out more than you can hope to recover from sales. Maybe your local camera club or artists' group could hold a competition on your behalf. If you want to use artwork that is not specially produced for your purpose, make sure you don't infringe the artist's or photographer's copyright. You can't use someone else's work without permission unless the originator has been dead for at least 50 years.

Getting the price right
Approach a reliable printer for a quote. You need someone who can produce good quality cards at reasonable prices. There might be such a

company in your locality, or you could get a quote from Abacus Colour Printers who offer a top-quality service at competitive charges.

As an example of Abacus's prices, here are the approximate charges (at the time of going to press) for full-colour greeting cards printed on quality 350gsm card with up to 50 printed words (typeset in black), with a choice of gloss or matt finish:

6 x 4in	First 1,000	£195	
			Standard rate: $2^1/_2$-3 weeks
	per extra 1,000	£130	
6 x 4in	First 1,000	£162	
			Reduced rate: 4-6 weeks
	per extra 1,000	£125	

Quantity discounts are available on the standard rate prices for orders of two or more different cards. VAT will be added at the current rate, and envelopes and postage are extra. Abacus also produce fine art reproductions of high quality. They'll send you full details of their services, with price lists and samples, on request.

Make your own
Hand-made cards sell well at fairs and bazaars. Christmassy embroidered motifs, miniature watercolours, pressed flowers are just a few of the varieties that make attractive and saleable cards.

The Craft Creations catalogue offers a range of greeting card blanks, with or without apertures, in various types of card: plain or embossed white, pale and strong colours, pearlised, glossy, metallic. . . Cards can be supplied with printed messages such as 'Merry Christmas', and generous discounts are given for quantity purchases. Craft Creations also sell the offcuts in mixed bags — these are the pieces punched from the centres of cards, and other trimmings. They can be made into attractive gift tags.

The Cutting Edge can supply greeting card blanks in a variety of styles, made from recycled paper.

For the children
It might be appropriate for your cause to promote a Christmas competition for local children to design and/or make a Christmas card. It's best if the competitors are divided into age groups — you can't expect similar standards from 6-year-olds and 16-year-olds. Your local paper will usually be delighted to help promote such a competition, but don't ask

them to help with the judging as their staff are unlikely to have the time.

Supporters' children might also like to help by making cards for you to sell at your Christmas Fair. Perhaps you could organise a few get-togethers for card-making sessions, where they could pool ideas. Robin Wright's book *How to Make Pop-Up Christmas Cards* provides ideas and instructions for cards that are easy to make and would be fun to receive. The book contains printed card for making six different cards, with ideas for more. You could use the designs provided as templates, and once the children see how to construct the cards they'll soon be producing their own original ideas. The potential is unlimited once the basic techniques are mastered. (*How to Make Pop-Up Birthday Cards* is also available in the same series.)

ONE MAN'S RUBBISH

In these environment-conscious times, people will respond positively to an enterprise aimed at conserving resources as well as raising money. There's money in old newspapers, used stamps, empty drinks cans and the like. Dealers in various kinds of 'waste' advertise in *Yellow Pages*.

PETER PAN PLAY PROJECT				
SPONSORED STEEL CAN COLLECTION				
Wash it and Squash it!				
Collector's name: Collector's address: Sponsorship form no:				
Sponsor's name	*Sponsor's address*	*Amount pledged per kilo of cans collected*	*Signed*	*Paid*

Figure 9. Example of a sponsorship form for an organised steel can collection

You could run a sponsored event that involves the collection of a specific type of waste material. For years people have responded generously by sponsoring swimmers, slimmers, cyclists and runners, but many feel that such events are something of a waste of time and energy which might be put to more productive use. A **sponsored waste collection** could be highly productive and more satisfying than walking round the park or swimming up and down a pool, worthy though such efforts are.

You would organise the event like any other sponsored affair, with each participant asking friends and family to pledge money payable on achievement of the target. The difference here would be that instead of pledging, say, 10 pence per mile or per length or per pound weight shed, they would pledge for example 10 pence per 100 grammes of used stamps or milk bottle tops or whatever. You then collect the pledged money as usual, but you can also add to that the money raised by selling the materials collected. Here are a few suggestions to start your group thinking:

- used postage stamps — British or foreign
- coins — foreign and old British
- old postcards
- books — paperback and hardback
- magazines and comics
- knitting wool
- aluminium milk bottle tops
- money-off coupons
- trading stamps
- waste paper, metal, glass and plastics for recycling.

If you like the idea of sponsored collecting but don't want to undertake selling the collected materials, you could send them to one of the many organisations who make use of them either by distributing items like unwanted furniture or by selling 'waste' to dealers. The Charities Aid Foundation publishes *Waste Not . . .*, a directory of such organisations listed regionally under the categories of material they welcome.

The Save-a-Can Scheme

According to the **Steel Can Recycling Information Bureau**, about half the drinks cans and virtually all food and petfood cans are made of steel (tinplate), and more than 1.125 billion (that is 1.125 thousand million) steel cans were recycled in the UK in 1990. Steel is the country's most recycled metal packaging material.

Is your local authority one of the 200 or so who already participate in the Save-a-Can Scheme by providing can banks where the public can deposit their 'washed and squashed' cans? If not, you might suggest they do. Save-a-Can makes a donation to a local charity for every tonne of cans collected — that charity could be yours.

The 1990 Environmental Protection Act introduced a system of Recycling Credits, at various monetary values, which the government hopes will help achieve its aim of recycling half of all recyclable household waste by the year 2000. It plans that charities and other local and community groups will benefit from these credits.

An information pack is available from the Steel Can Recycling Information Bureau, who also have a video about the Save-a-Can Scheme available on loan. You can also contact Save-a-Can direct, and they'll send you a list of established Save-a-Can sites.

THE LONDON MARATHON

There's no doubt that this annual event has acquired a glamour that no other race in the country can touch. If you can find a marathon runner, man or woman, who'll run for your cause, you'll be on a financial winner.

Such is the race's fame that you could probably persuade a local business to underwrite your runner's expenses through sponsorship in return for the publicity the event attracts (see the Social Sponsorship section in Chapter 5, Help from Industry and Commerce).

Fund-raising for your cause is done through the better known kind of sponsorship, where people pledge specific amounts of money per mile run or according to the time in which the run is completed.

A runner who is particularly appropriate to your cause in, say, age or occupation gives an additional interest to the event. A recent illustration of this was provided by Allan Campbell of Carlisle, who ran in the 1991 London Marathon to raise funds for the association which helps sufferers of the painful and crippling bone illness Paget's Disease. The disease mainly affects older people, and Allan Campbell's efforts on the society's behalf drew a tremendous response. He's a 58-year-old grandfather and he ran the full distance in a time of three hours 38 minutes, raising more than £7,300. He had never done any running until 1981, when he decided to act on Department of Health warnings about the nation's unfitness. His first run for charity was the Cumbrian Run, a half-marathon which he ran in 1982, and he's been running on behalf of good causes ever since.

Till his 1991 run, Allan had done most of the sponsored fund-raising himself with the help of family and friends, and when Tricia Orton,

Administrator for The National Association for the Relief of Paget's Disease, asked if he would run on their behalf, he was more than willing but had doubts about the fund-raising aspect. He had been finding that 'people were not as forthcoming as they used to be', a problem intensified by the shortage of money all round. However, Tricia and the society's members undertook the fund-raising, leaving Allan free to concentrate on the run. The joint enterprise was a huge success.

Allan offers a couple of tips to swell the funds raised from sponsored events:

- number all the sponsorship forms, and offer a chance in a lucky draw to all helpers who bring back a form with more than £5;
- find a local company willing to donate a prize for whoever collects the largest amount of sponsorship money.

It's wonderful what an additional incentive can achieve, Allan says.

The next marathon he plans to run will be the 1993 London Marathon. He'll then be 60 years old, and aims to make it a really big fund-raising effort, involving as many people as he can muster to help.

THE MAYOR'S APPEAL

It's traditional in many towns and cities that the Mayor heads a charity appeal which is on-going throughout his or her term of office. The Mayor's Appeal usually raises money in support of one or more specific local causes. The official fund-raising will probably include one or two large events, like a gala concert, a dinner dance or a garden party, and will be augmented by contributions from events held by other individuals and groups.

You could lobby the council, particularly the councillor who is in line to be the next mayor, to include your cause among those which will benefit from the appeal. Make your approaches well in advance, as there will be many other applicants.

AN AUCTION OF PROMISES

This is different from the usual type of auction where bids are made for goods on display. Here we have pledges offered to the highest bidder. These pledges can be for just about anything a donor feels able to offer — goods, services, unusual activities, instruction, entertainment. . . anything goes.

The method of bidding is the same as in a conventional auction, with 'lots' put up in numerical order according to the prepared catalogue, where instead of the normal lots, the promises and their donors' names are set out. If you can persuade an experienced auctioneer to conduct the bidding, so much the better — things will move along quickly and smoothly.

A very successful example of an auction of promises was held one summer evening in 1991 by the Parochial Church Council of Milton Lilbourne in Wiltshire. The event raised £1,500, which was divided between the Salisbury Cathedral Spire Appeal and St Peter's Church, Milton Lilbourne, organ repairs. The catalogue included such varied pledges as:

- a half-hour trial lesson in a single engine light aircraft
- two hours weeding
- dinner for two in a local pub
- a magnum of champagne
- three hours baby-sitting
- a complete car valeting
- a six-pound Christmas cake for Christmas 1991
- transport for up to three people to visit anywhere within 100 miles, returning the same day
- a cookery lesson
- a hamper of home-made jam and cakes
- a drive in a vintage Bentley
- a voucher for an interior furnishing shop
- one-and-a-half hours dog walking
- two hours use of a tennis court
- a cut-and-blow or a cut-and-set at a local hair salon
- ten pounds of marmalade for the following January
- lunch at the House of Lords plus a tour of the Palace of Westminster

Altogether, 63 'lots' were offered.

Your programme should set out some guidelines about arranging for the fulfilment of promises, and should state that normal auction rules apply. For example:

- lots become the responsibility of the purchaser as soon as the hammer falls
- all lots purchased must be paid for at the auction
- donors should be notified of the successful bidder
- the purchaser should make direct contact with the donor to make

mutually convenient arrangements for the fulfilment of the promise — the organisers cannot take responsibility for this.

Silent table
In addition to the auction itself, the Milton Lilbourne event included a 'silent table'. This is simply a table set out with small items on to which a bidder adds a price, with the item eventually going to whoever makes the highest bid. The silent table offered such items as:

- a sponge cake
- a fruit cake
- home-made jam
- a basket of sweets
- a box of assorted herbs
- clay pots
- two bottles of wine.

By including a silent table, the organisers ensured that the scope for donations was so wide that everyone could contribute regardless of their means.

The silent table is an idea that could be incorporated into other events, too. It takes up little room, requires no one's constant attendance, and will intrigue because it's just a little bit different. Try it, for example, at a theme party, and stock it with small items in keeping with the rest of the party.

GARDENS ON DISPLAY

Town gardens, suburban gardens, country gardens... Gardening and plant enthusiasts will happily pay up for a chance to browse around other people's gardens — or even window boxes, if these are something special. Pot up some cuttings and offer them for sale; compile a list of your plants, with tips on cultivation, and offer copies for sale. Add to the profits by selling tea, coffee, soft drinks, cakes and biscuits, and if you have the space to let people sit down, the Olde Worlde English Cream Tea is a real money-maker. This is an event that could run for a day, a week, even a fortnight if you can round up enough gardeners to keep it running.

BLANKET COLLECTION

Your local football club might be willing to let you hold a blanket collection, where a team of people circles the field during the interval, holding a blanket open at its corners while spectators throw money into it. You need one or two agile people following the bianket, too, to pick up coins that miss the target. An announcement on the public address system just before kick-off, repeated as soon as the first half ends, tells the crowd what the collection is for. You'll need a room in which to sort out, tot up and bag the money ready for banking.

FRUGAL LUNCH

Invite a number of people to 'lunch', for which they pay the average price of a restaurant lunch but eat only a very small amount of food, for example a small bowl of soup and a bread roll. The difference in cost goes to your fund. (Very popular with slimmers.)

CHILDREN'S CLOTHING EXCHANGE

Best held at weekends or at a time when the children can come along with a parent, this is a sale of children's outgrown garments. You can make a flat handling charge per garment, or a fee per 'exchange' made, or a percentage of the selling price.

WISHING WELL

Erect a wishing well at almost any event and watch the money splash in. You need a sturdy waterproof vessel: a barrel (or half barrel), a heavy plastic tub, a bin. . . Put stones, bricks or other weights in the bottom for stability, then lay a base of dark plastic and scatter a few coins in as 'bait'. Include some silver, which will shine invitingly through the water. Mount a 'roof' and decorate it with ribbons, balloons and a banner bearing your cause's name and logo, and the words 'Wishing Well'.

SELL ADVERTISING SPACE

You can offset the production costs — and perhaps make a profit, too — by selling advertising space in your publications. Such publications might include newsletters and magazines, annual reports, calendars, brochures, events programmes. . . just about anything that will have a substantial readership.

The Directory of Social Change publication *Sell Space to Make Money* by Audrey Semple explains how to do this, giving detailed procedures, examples, and many ideas.

FASHION SHOW

Ask a local fashion shop (or a clothing manufacturer if there's one in your area) to help you stage a fashion show. Plan this thoroughly so that you can exploit all its money-making possibilities like programme advertising, advance ticket sales and a raffle.

You need:

1. A venue big enough to accommodate a 'catwalk' but intimate enough to give the whole audience a clear view of the clothes shown.
2. Refreshment facilities. You can either cost light refreshments into your ticket price or offer them for sale at the interval.
3. A mobile disco to provide the necessary music. Operators advertise in local papers and Yellow Pages.
4. Good lighting.
5. A sound system with microphone for the fashion commentary and announcements.
6. The services of a hairdresser/beautician, to give the 'professional' touch to your models.
7. Models to show the clothes. The shop or company might arrange this, or you could recruit your models from volunteers, from theatrical groups, from local Beauty Queen contestants, from a sixth form college — just a few possibilities.

   One way to add an intriguing dimension to your show is to incorporate the help of a slimming club. Successful slimmers modelling fashionable clothes: what a great publicity bonus for the slimming club as well as for your event.

Be sure to give everyone concerned warm acknowledgement in your programme and in subsequent press reports. Don't forget to give the local paper plenty of notice, and to take photographs yourselves in case they're needed. (Perhaps, too, your models would be interested in buying prints of their moment of glory.)

PAPERBACK BOOK SALE

Easier to organise than a full-scale book fair, this could be held either in a local hall or in a private house. Arrange the books in categories: Crime and Thriller, Romance, Children's, Non-fiction and so on. Put a flat price on whole categories if you can, rather than on individual books. This saves work for the organisers, and means that the customers don't have to search or ask for prices.

For a sale in a public hall, you can advertise the event as widely as you like, and ask for books to be donated. However, if you're using a private home it's best to keep to an 'invitation only' policy for security reasons, so you'll probably have to allow more time to accumulate stock through people you plan to invite.

If you have the accommodation, sell light refreshments to supplement your profits. You might light to run a small raffle, too.

AFTERNOON TEA PARTY

As a novelty and a change from a coffee morning, you could hold a traditional tea party. Keep the number of guests to a level you can accommodate comfortably. One of the joys of a tea party is that everyone can sit down and relax. Dust off your best china — no mugs or beakers on this occasion — and borrow more from friends. Most people have a china tea-set safely put away for special occasions. Serve wafer-thin sandwiches with delicate fillings, scones with butter and jam, fairy cakes, iced dainties.

You might also offer a choice of teas, with lemon as an alternative to milk.

Price the tickets around what it would cost to have an elegant afternoon tea at a good hotel. If you can persuade friends to contribute most of the goodies, you should be able to show a healthy profit.

SCHOOL PROJECT

One of your local schools might be willing to adopt your cause as a fund-raising project. Many heads are keen to promote a community spirit among their pupils. A committee of senior pupils could take responsibility for organising, promoting and running a week of event son school premises (with the Head's consent and cooperation, of course), liaising with your own committee to make sure that legal and safety aspects are covered (and to see that nothing too outrageous is planned).

Glossary

agenda: a programme of business for a meeting.

advertising: publicity that is paid for.

audit: an examination of accounts by an authorised person.

budget: a planned programme of income and expenditure.

car boot sale: an open-air sale where the public can park cars and vans for the purpose of selling surplus or unwanted goods direct from their vehicles.

cash book: a notebook recording a detailed summary of money received and money paid out.

charitable status: the status of being registered with the Charity Commission as an officially recognised and accountable charity.

collectables: items which originally had little or no value but which are now sought after by collectors, sometimes commanding prices far beyond their material worth. (For example, football medals and programmes, commemorative plates, tobacco tins, cigarette packets.)

concession stall: a stall where goods are sold principally for the stall-holder's profit, with a fee or an agreed percentage of profits being paid to the charity running the event.

constitution: a set of rules governing an organisation's objectives and activities.

contingency fund: an amount of money set aside to meet unexpected needs not catered for in the budget.

covering letter: a letter sent with, for example, a document, to identify the sender, to explain the purpose of the document, and as a courteous contact with the addressee.

deadline: a specified time or date by which a job should be done.

deed of covenant: a legal document; a written agreement under which one person promises to make a series of payments to another person or to an organisation for nothing in return. It is binding on the person who makes the promise.

donation: a sum of money or a gift given to a charitable organisation.

131

donor: a person who gives a donation.

form: condition of fitness and ability.

Gift Aid: a scheme by which individuals and companies receive tax relief on gifts to charity of money over a specified sum.

gifts in kind: items given by a company to a charity, for example office furniture, raw materials, end-of-lines, products for use as prizes.

goodwill: the established popularity and trustworthiness of a business or other enterprise. In business, goodwill is a marketable asset.

grant-making trust: a body which exists to manage and distribute funds for the benefit of others.

handout: something given free of charge, for example an information sheet.

imprint: the name and address of the publisher or printer of books, magazines, brochures and so on.

Inter-Library Loan Service: a system by which any book in print in the UK can be obtained for a library user. Their local branch library orders the book through the British Lending Library, usually making a small charge for the service.

liaison officer: a person forming a link with another unit, department or organisation.

logo: (abbreviation of logotype) a design, emblem or trademark.

lottery: any arrangement where the distribution of prizes or benefits is the result of chance and not of skill or judgement.

minutes: a written record of proceedings and of decisions taken at meetings.

parochial charities: charities restricted or confined to work or to distribute benefits within their parish boundaries.

payroll giving schemes: schemes enabling employees to give to charity directly from their pay and to get tax relief on the payments.

press release: a prepared statement issued to the media for publicity purposes.

product endorsement: publicly expressed approval of a product by an individual, company or organisation whose recommendation is likely to influence the success of that product.

product link: a connection between what a company produces and a cause or event the company might sponsor or otherwise support.

professional fund-raiser: a person or company whose business is the raising of funds on behalf of an organisation which employs them on a fee-paying or a percentage of profits basis.

promotional merchandise: items bearing an organisation's name and/or logo, sold to make money and promote public awareness of that organisation. Can include, for example, button badges, carrier bags, pens and pencils, T-shirts.

QUANGO: acronym of 'quasi-autonomous non-governmental organisation'. An official but non-governmental organisation empowered to spend government money. For example, The Arts Council, the English Tourist Board.

quorum: a minimum number of people who must be present to enable the transaction of business.

recycling credits: a scheme in which the savings in disposal or collection costs of materials for recycling are passed back to the recycler. Local authorities receiving such credits are empowered to pay part or all of the savings to third parties.

secondee: a member of a company's staff temporarily placed with a charitable organisation to work on the organisation's behalf (see 'secondment'.)

secondment: a temporary transfer of a member of staff from a company to work for a charity, the secondee continuing to receive normal salary from the company, with the charity usually meeting any other expenses arising from the job.

social sponsorship: the payment of a fee or provision of a service by one organisation to another with which it has no direct connection, in the hope and expectation of benefit from publicity, advertising, the generation of public goodwill and so on.

template: an outline pattern from which a shape can be traced and cut out in card or other material.

thrift shop: another name for a charity shop.

tombola: a lottery in which the public buy tickets drawn at random from a box or drum which contains both winning and losing numbers.

Tonne: a metric ton = 1,000 kilogrammes.

totalisator tax: a tax imposed by the Inland Revenue on stakes invested in betting on a totalisator (tote).

tote: an automatic betting machine.

trustee: a person to whom the management of funds is committed for the benefit of others.

umbrella fund: a fund covering a variety of activities, usually related to a common or complementary purpose.

Booklets and Leaflets

THE CHARITY COMMISSION FOR ENGLAND AND WALES EXPLANATORY LEAFLETS

CC27   *Provision of Alcohol on Charity Premises*
CC28   *Selling Charity Land*
CC29   *Charities and Local Authorities*
CC31   *Educational Charities*
CC31   *Acquiring Land*
CC34   *Official Custodian for Charities: Sales and Purchases*
CC36   *Making a Scheme*
CC38   *Capital Expenditure by Charity Trustees*
CC39   *Extraordinary Repair Funds*
CC40   *Disaster Appeals — Attorney General's Guidelines*
CC41   *Payment of Charity Trustees*
AC7   *Charity Accounts; Notes for Charity Trustees*
073   *Investment Principles*
RE4   *Central Register of Charities*
RE4(R) *Registration of Religious Charities*
TP1   *Trustee Investments Act 1961*
200   *A Statement of Recommended Practice of Accounting by Charities: A Résumé*
201   *The Social Fund; Charities for the Relief of the Poor*
1034   *The Commissioners' South West Regional Office*
1039   *Availability of Central Register Files (London)*

Copies of these leaflets are available free of charge from:
    The Charity Commission
    St Alban's House
    57-60 Haymarket
    London SW1Y 4QX
Requests for leaflets should be accompanied by a self-addressed stamped envelope no smaller than 10 x 8 in. (List reproduced by permission.)

INLAND REVENUE LEAFLETS (free from your local tax office)

1HT3   *An Introduction to Inheritance Tax*
IR74   *Deeds of Covenant — Getting It Right for Tax*
IR113   *A Guide for Donors and Charities*
IR64   *Giving to Charity — How Businesses Can Get Tax Relief*
IR65   *Giving to Charity — How Individuals Can Get Tax Relief*
IR46   *Income Tax and Corporation Tax — Clubs, Societies and Associations*
1HT1   *Inheritance Tax*
IR75   *Tax Reliefs for Charities*

DIRECTORY OF SOCIAL CHANGE

Fund-raising notes, currently 95 pence each or £7.95 for the set of 12:
Developing a Strategy
Doing Research
Drawing up a Budget
Earning Money
Fund-Raising sources
Organising an Appeal
Organising an Event
Planning a Capital Project
Raising Money Locally
Setting Up
Social Sponsorship
Writing an Application

OTHER USEFUL BOOKLETS AND LEAFLETS

The Giving Business £3 from Business Matters (The Giving Business), BBC Education, London W12 7RJ.

Negotiating Grants: issues for local authorities and voluntary groups, £1 from Action with Communities in Rural England (ACRE), Somerford Court, Somerford Road, Cirencester, Glos GL7 1TW.

The Nuclear Weapons Connection: a guide to UK companies' links with nuclear weapons, £2 from Ethical Investment Research Service (EIRIS), 504 Bondway Business Centre, 71 Bondway, London SW8 1SQ.

Organising a Carnival or Gala 75p from the National Federation of Community Organisations, 8-9 Upper Street, London N1 0PQ.

Parish Appraisals Pack £5 (half price to parish or community groups), from ACRE (see above).

Rural Advice and Information: setting up a local service, £1.50 from ACRE (see above)

Directory of National Charitable Guilds and Trusts £2 from ACRE (see above).

The Single Market: Toy Safety, Department of Trade and Industry free from Trading Standards Offices.

Social Sponsorship in Action £1.50 from Action Match, Canning Town Public Hall, 105 Barking Road, London E16 4HQ.

Periodicals

Antiquarian Book Monthly Review
Suite G, Bullingdon House, 174B Cowley Road, Oxford OX4 1UE. Tel: (0865) 794704. Fax: (0865) 794582. £1.80 monthly, UK subscription £22 per annum.

Book and Magazine Collector
43-45 St Mary's Road, Ealing, London W5 5RQ. Tel: (081) 579 1082. £1.85 monthly, from newsagents.

Charity
Charities Aid Foundation, 48 Pembury Road, Tonbridge, Kent TN9 2JD. Monthly, annual subscription £30 (incl p&p). Single issue £1.75 (plus p&p).

The Craftsman Magazine
PO Box 5, Lowthorpe, Driffield, East Yorks YO25 8SD. Tel: (0377) 45213. Fax: (0377) 45730. £1.25 bi-monthly from newsagents.

Essentials
GE Magazines Ltd, Garden House, 57-59 Long Acre, London WC2E 9JL. Tel: (071) 836 0519. Fax: (071) 836 0280.

The Ethical Investor
Quarterly Newsletter published by The Ethical Investment Research Service. Subscription £8 per annum.

Family Circle
King's Reach Tower, Stamford Street, London SE1 9LS. Tel: (071) 261 5000. Fax: (071) 261 5929.

Prima
Portland House, Stag Place, London SW1E 5AU. Tel: (071) 245 8700.

Popular Crafts
Argus Specialist Publications, Argus House, Boundary Way, Hemel
Hempstead, Herts HP2 7ST. Tel: (0442) 66551. Monthly £1.60.

Radio Times
BBC Enterprises, 35 Marylebone High Street, London W1M 4AA. Tel:
(071) 580 5577.

Rural Viewpoint
News magazine published by Action With Communities in Rural England. £1.50 (incl p & p) for a copy of the latest issue. UK subscription
£7.50 per annum (six issues).

Voluntary Voice
Published by the London Voluntary Services Council. Subscription rates
on application.

Woman and Home
IPC Magazines Ltd, King's Reach Tower, Stamford Street, London SE1
9LS. Tel: (071) 261 5423.

Woman's Realm
IPC Magazines Ltd, King's Reach Tower, Stamford Street, London SE1
9LS. Tel: (071) 261 5000.

Woman's Weekly
IPC Magazines Ltd, King's Reach Tower, Stamford Street, London SE1
9LS. Tel: (071) 261 6131. Fax: (071) 261 6322.

World's Fair
2 Daltry Street, Oldham, Lancs. Tel: (061) 624 3687.

Books

A Guide to Company Giving The Directory of Social Change, 1991, £14.95.

A Guide To Gift Aid, Michael Norton, The Directory of Social Change, 1991, £7.95.

A Guide to Grants for Individuals in Need The Directory of Social Change, 1990, £12.95.

A Practical Guide to Company Law for Voluntary Organisations Bev Cross, The Directory of Social Change, 1991, £5.95.

Arts Funding Guide, The Ed. Anne-Marie Doulton, The Directory of Social Change, 1991, £12.50.

Barbecues Carole Handslip, Merehurst Press, 1991, £2.45.

Beautiful Patchwork Gifts Linda Seward, Cassell, 1991, £9.95.

Broadcast Charitable Appeals Diana Leat, The Directory of Social Change, 1990, £5.95.

Business and Environmental Groups: A Natural Partnership? Susan Forrester, The Directory of Social Change, 1990, £9.95.

But Is It Legal? Fund-Raising and the Law Sally Capper, Bedford Square Press, 1988, £2.95.

Central Government Grants Guide Annually from The Directory of Social Change, £7.95.

Charitable Status: A Practical Handbook Andrew Phillips, The Directory of Social Change, 1988, £5.95.

Charity Accounting and Taxation R.G. Vincent, Butterworths, 1991, £37.50.

Charity Christmas Cards: How to Produce Them, How to Sell Them, How to Make Money from Them Hilary Blume, Charities Advisory Trust, 1984, £3.95.

Children's Party Cakes Carole Handslip, Ebury Press, 1991, £6.99.

Colour for Men Carole Jackson, Piatkus Books, £8.95.

Colour Me Beautiful Carole Jackson, Piatkus Books, £7.95.

Colour Me Beautiful Makeup Book Carole Jackson, Piatkus Books, £7.95.

Complete Style Guide from Colour Me Beautiful Mary Spillane, Piatkus Books, 1991, £14.95.

Desserts Mandy Wagstaff, Merehurst, 1991, £2.45.

Dinosaur Cakes Jacqui Hine, Merehurst, 1991, £9.99.

Directory of Grant-making Trusts regularly updated, Charities Aid Foundation, £50 approx.

Easy to Make Knitted Toys Joy Gammon, Anaya, 1990, £8.99.

Easy to Patchwork Lynette Mostaghimi, Anaya, 1991, £8.99.

Educational Grants Directory The Directory of Social Change, 1991, £14.95.

Environmental Grants The Directory of Social Change, 1991, £12.50.

Family Circle Beautiful Things to Make for Baby J.B. Fairfax, 1990, £2.99.

Family Circle Best Selling Food & Craft J.B. Fairfax, 1990, £2.99.

Family Circle Kids' Knits and Crochet J.B. Fairfax, 1990, £2.99.

Family Circle Soft Toys to Sew, J.B. Fairfax, £2.99.

Festive Food of America, The Martina Nicolls, Kyle Cathie, 1991, £4.99.

Festive Food of China, The Deh-Ta-Hsiung, Kyle Cathie, 1991, £4,99.

Festive Food of England, The Henrietta Green, Kyle Cathie, 1991, £4.99.

Festive Food of France, The Marie-Pierre Moine, Kyle Cathie, 1991, £4.99.

Festive Food of Italy, The Maddalena Bonino, Kyle Cathie, 1991, £4.99.

Festive Food of Spain, The Nicholas Butcher, Kyle Cathie, 1991, £4.99.

Finding Sponsors for Community Projects Caroline Gillies, The Directory of Social Change/Friends of the Earth, 1990, £7.95.

Fundraising and Grant Making: a Case Study of ITV Telethon '88 Diana Leat, Charities Aid Foundation, 1989, £7.95.

Getting Ready for Contracts Richard Macfarlane and Sandy Adirondack, The Directory of Social Change, 1991, £7.95.

Government Grants: A Guide for Voluntary Organisations Maggie Jones, Bedford Square Press, 6th Edition, 1991, £6.95.

Grants from Europe Ann Davison and Bill Seary, Bedford Square Press, 6th Edition, 1990, £7.95.

How to Make Pop-Up Birthday Cards Robin Wright, Kingfisher Books, 1991, £2.95.

How to Make Pop-Up Christmas Cards Robin Wright, Kingfisher Books, 1991, £2.95.

Jumble Sale Handbook, The Frances Pitt, Century, 1991, £4.99.

Just About Managing: a guide to Effective Management for Voluntary Organisations and Community Groups Sandy Merritt Adirondack, London Voluntary Service Council, 1989, £7.50 + £1 p & p.

The London Grants Guide The Directory of Social Change, 1991, £9.95.

Major Companies and Their Charitable Giving Ed. Dave Casson, The Directory of Social Change, 1991, £14.95.

Making Silk Flowers Anne Hamilton and Kathleen White, Merehurst, 1990, £6.95.

Miniature Novelty Cakes Lindsay John Bradshaw, Merehurst, 1991, £6.99.

Pizza Book, The Evelyne Slomon, Robert Hale, 1991, £7.95.

Publisher's Freelance Directory, The annually, Hobsons, £30 approx.

Rag Doll Handbook, The Ana Lakeland, Batsford, 1991, £14.99.

Raising Money from Industry Michael Norton, The Directory of Social Change, 1989, £5.95.

Sell Space to Make Money Audrey Semple, The Directory of Social Change, 1987, £2.95.

Showman's Directory annually, Lance Publications, £7.50.

Socially Responsible Investment Sue Ward, The Directory of Social Change, 1991, £7.95.

Sources of Charity Finance Ed. Norman Lee, Charities Aid Foundation, £12.95 inc. p. & p.

Sugarpaste Christmas Cakes Anne Smith, Merehurst, 1989, £8.95.

Tolley's Charities Manual looseleaf format, regularly updated, Tolley Publishing, £49.95.

Voluntary but Not Amateur: A Guide to the Law for Voluntary Organisations and Community Groups Duncan Forbes, Ruth Haynes and Jacki Reason, London Voluntary Service Council, 3rd Edition, 1990, £7.95 + £1 p. & p.

Waste not . . . Charities Aid Foundation, £3.95.

Writers' & Artists' Yearbook annually, A. & C. Black, £8.95.

Publishers

Anaya Publishers Ltd, 3rd Floor, Strode House, 44-50 Osnaburgh Street, London NW1 3ND. Tel: (071) 383 2997. Fax: (071) 383 3076.

B.T. Batsford Ltd, 4 Fitzhardinge Street, London W1H 0AH. Tel (071) 486 8484. Fax: (071) 487 4296.

Bedford Square Press, National Council for Voluntary Organisations, 26 Bedford Square, London WC1B 3HU. Tel: (071) 636 4066. Fax: (071) 254 5325.

Black, A & C, PLC, 35 Bedford Row, London WC1R 4JH. Tel: (071) 242 0946. Fax: (071) 831 8478.

Butterworth Law Publishers Ltd, 88 Kingsway, London WC2B 6AB. Tel: (071) 405 6900. Fax: (071) 405 1332.

Cassell PLC, Villiers House, 41/47 Strand, London WC2N 5JE. Tel: (071) 839 4900. Fax: (071) 839 1804.

Century Publishing Ltd, Random Century House, 20 Vauxhall Bridge Road, London SW1V 2SA. Tel: (071) 973 9670. Fax: (071) 233 6125.

Charities Advisory Trust, 9 Mansfield Place, London NW3 1HS. Tel: (071) 435 6523.

Charities Aid Foundation, 48 Pembury Road, Tonbridge, Kent TN9 2JD. Tel: (0732) 771333.

The Directory of Social Change, Radius Works, Back Lane, London NW3 1HL. Tel: (071) 284 4364.

Ebury Press, Random Century House, 20 Vauxhall Bridge Road, London SW1V 2SA. Tel: (071) 973 9690. Fax: (071) 233 6057.

J.B. Fairfax Press Ltd, 9 Trinity Centre, Park Farm Estate, Wellingborough, Northants NN8 6ZB. Tel: (0933) 402330. Fax: (0933) 402234.

Robert Hale, Clerkenwell House, 45-47 Clerkenwell Green, London EC1R 0HT. Tel: (071) 251 2661. Fax: (071) 490 4958.

Hobsons Publishing PLC, Bateman Street, Cambridge CB2 1LZ. Tel: (0223) 354551. Fax: (0223) 323154.

Kingfisher Books, Grisewood and Dempsey Ltd, Elsley House, 24-30

Great Titchfield Street, London W1P 7AD. Tel: (071) 631 0878. Fax: (071) 323 4694.

Kyle Cathie Ltd, 3 Vincent Square, London SW1P 2LX. Tel: (071) 834 8027. Fax: (071) 821 9258.

Lance Publications, Brook House, Mint Street, Godalming, Surrey GU7 1HE. Tel: (0483) 422184. Fax: (0483) 425697.

London Voluntary Service Council, 68 Chalton Street, London NW1 1JR. Tel: (071) 388 0241. Fax: (071) 387 2191.

Merehurst Ltd, Ferry House, 51/57 Lacy Road, Putney, London SW15 1PR. Tel: (081) 780 1177. Fax: (081) 780 1714.

Piatkus Books, 5 Windmill Street, London W1P 1HF. Tel: (071) 631 0710. Fax: (071) 436 7137.

Tolley Publishing Co Ltd, Tolley House, 5 Addiscombe Road, Croydon, Surrey CR9 5AF. Tel: (081) 686 9141. Fax: (081) 686 3155/(081) 760 0588.

Addresses

GOVERNMENT DEPARTMENTS AND OTHER OFFICIAL ORGANISATIONS

Arts Council of Great Britain, 14 Great Peter Street, London SW1 3NQ. Tel: (071) 333 0100. Fax: (071) 973 6590.

British Broadcasting Corporation, Broadcasting House, Portland Place, London W1A 1AA. Tel: (071) 580 4468.

British Film Institute, 21 Stephen Street, London W1P 1PL. Tel: (071) 255 1444. Fax: (071) 436 7950.

Commission for Racial Equality, Elliot House, 10-12 Allington Street, London SW1E 5EH. Tel: (071) 828 7022. Fax: (071) 630 7605.

Countryside Commission Central Offices, John Dower House, Crescent Place, Cheltenham, Glos GL50 3RA. Tel: (0242) 521381 Fax: (0242) 584270.

Crafts Council (Grants and Services Section), 1 Oxendon Street, London SW1Y 4AU. Tel: (071) 930 4811. Fax: (071) 321 0427.

Data Protection Registrar, Springfield House, Water Lane, Wilmslow, Cheshire SK9 5AX. Tel: (0625) 535711.

Department of Education and Science, Elizabeth House, York Road, London SE1 7PH. Tel: (071) 934 9000. Fax: (071) 934 9082.

Department of the Environment, 2 Marsham Street, London SW1P 3EB. Tel: (071) 276 4432. Fax: (071) 276 0818.

Department of Health, Alexander Fleming House, London SE1 6BY. Tel: (071) 407 5522.

Department of Trade and Industry, 1 Victoria Street, London SW1H 0ET. Tel: (071) 215 5000.

English Heritage, Fortress House, 23 Savile Row, London W1X 1AB. Tel: (071) 973 3000.

Equal Opportunities Commission, Overseas House, Quay Street, Manchester M3 3HN. Tel: (061) 833 9244.

European Parliament London Office, 2 Queen Anne's Gate, London SW1H 9AA. Tel: (071) 222 0411.

Gaming Board for Great Britain, Berkshire House, 168-173 High Holborn, London WC1V 7AA. Tel: (071) 240 0821.

Home Office Voluntary Services Unit, 50 Queen Anne's Gate, London SW1H 9AT. Tel: (071) 273 2537.

Independent Broadcasting Authority, 70 Brompton Road, London SW3. Tel: (071) 584 7011.

Inland Revenue Claims Branch, Charity Division (England, Wales and Northern Ireland), St John's House, Merton Road, Bootle, Merseyside L69 9BB. Tel: (051) 922 6363.

Inland Revenue Claims Branch, Charity Division (Scotland), Trinity Park House, South Trinity Road, Edinburgh, Scotland EH3 3SD. Tel: (031) 522 6255.

Nature Conservancy Council, Northminster House, Peterborough, Cambs PE1 1UA. Tel: (0733) 40345. Fax: (0733) 68834.

Office of Population Censuses and Surveys, St Catherine's House, 10 Kingsway, London WC2. Tel: (071) 242 0262. Library tel: (071) 242 0262 Ext 2268. Open to the public Mon-Fri 9am - 4pm.

The Sports Council for England, 16 Upper Woburn Place, London WC1H 0QP. Tel: (071) 388 1277. Fax: (071) 383 5740.

CHARITABLE ORGANISATIONS

Action Match (Community Sponsorship Development Agency), Canning Town Public Hall. 105 Barking Road, London E16 4HQ. Tel: (071) 473 2270.

Action Resource Centre, 1st Floor, 102 Park Village East, London NW1 3SP. Tel: (071) 383 2200. Fax: (071) 383 3332.

Action with Communities in Rural England (ACRE), Somerford Court, Somerford Road, Cirencester, Glos GL7 1TW. Tel: (0285) 653477.

Charities Advisory Trust, 9 Mansfield Place, London NW3 1HS. Tel: (071) 435 6523.

Charities Aid Foundation, 48 Pembury Road, Tonbridge, Kent TN9 2JD. Tel: (0732) 771333.

Charity Christmas Card Council (4Cs), 49 Lamb's Conduit Street, London WC1N 3NG. Tel: (071) 242 0546. Fax: (071) 242 1903.

The Charity Commission, St Alban's House, 57-60 Haymarket, London SW1Y 4QX. Tel: (071) 210 4405.

The Charity Commission, Graeme House, Derby Square, Liverpool L2 7SB. Tel: (051) 227 3191. Fax: (051) 255 0971.

The Charity Commission, The Deane, Tangier, Taunton, Somerset TA1 4AY. Tel: (0823) 345000.

Council for Voluntary Service, St Thomas Centre, Ardwick Green North, Manchester M12 6FZ. Tel: (061) 273 3837. (See National Association of Councils for Voluntary Service).

Friends of the Earth, 26-28 Underwood street, London N1 7JQ. Tel: (071) 490 1555. Fax: (071) 490 0881.

Imperial Cancer Research Fund, PO Box 123, Lincoln's Inn Fields, London WC2A 3PX. Tel: (071) 242 0200.

InterChange Advisory Service, InterChange Studios, 15 Wilkin Street, London NW5 3NG. Tel: (071) 267 9421. Fax: (071) 482 5292.

London Voluntary Service Council, 68 Chalton Street, London NW1 1JR. Tel: (071) 388 0241. Fax: (071) 387 2191.

National Association of Councils for Voluntary Service, PO Box 717, Sheffield, South Yorkshire S1 1NL. Tel: (0742) 786636.

National Council for Voluntary Organisations, 26 Bedford Square, London WC1B 3HU. Tel: (071) 636 4066. Fax: (071) 436 3188.

National Federation of Community Organisations, 8-9 Upper Street, London N1 0PQ. Tel: (071) 226 0189.

Retired Executives Action Clearing-House (REACH), 89 Southwark Street, London SE1 0HD. Tel: (071) 928 0452. Fax: (071) 928 0798.

Scottish Council for Voluntary Organisations, 18-19 Claremont Crescent, Edinburgh, Scotland EH7 4QD. Tel: (031) 556 3882. Fax: (031) 556 0279.

OTHER ASSOCIATIONS

British Actors Equity Association, 8 Harley Street, London W1N 2AB. Tel: (071) 636 6367. Fax: (071) 637 9311.

British Insurance Brokers Association, BIBA House, 14 Bevis Marks, London EC3A 7NT. Tel: (071) 623 9043.

Entertainment Agents Association, 04 Keyes House, Dolphin Square, London SW1V 3NA. Tel: (071) 834 0515.

Musicians Union, 60-62 Clapham Road, London SW9 0JJ. Tel: (071) 582 5566. Fax: (071) 582 9805.

The National Association for the Relief of Paget's Disease, Administrator: Tricia Orton, The Department of Medicine, University of Manchester, Hope Hospital, Salford M6 8HD. Tel: (061) 787 4949. Fax: (061) 787 4344.

Performing Right Society, 29-33 Berners Street, London W1P 4AA. Tel: (071) 580 5544. Fax: (071) 631 4138.

Provincial Booksellers Fairs Association (PBFA)., The Old Coach House, 16 Melbourn Street, Royston, Herts SG8 7BZ. Tel: (0763) 248400.

AGENTS AND CONSULTANTS

Book Fairs, Jill Trenholme, 45 Park Road, Hale, Cheshire WA15 9LS.

Colour Me Beautiful (headquarters UK, Europe, Africa and Middle East), Joint Managing Director Mary Spillane, 56 Abbey Business Centre, Ingate Place, London SW8 3NS. Tel: (071) 627 5211.

Colour Me Beautiful, Consultant Mac Tompsett, Westwood, Vicarage Lane, Gresford, Near Wrexham, Clwyd LL12 8US. Tel: (0978) 852816.

Crafts and Collectors' Fairs, Jean M. Harris, Lane Side Farm, Hawksworth Lane, Hawksworth, Guiseley, Yorks LS20 8HD. Tel: (0943) 76804.

First Division Marketing, Consultant Caroline Gillies, Southlea House, Ellington Road, Maidenhead, Berks SL6 0AX. Tel: (0628) 27613. Fax: (0628) 25524.

Johnny Howard Associates Ltd, The Folly, Pinner Hill Road, Pinner, Middlesex HA5 3YQ. Tel: (081) 429 2822. Fax: (081) 868 6497.

Barbara Keeley-Huggett, Independent Consultant, 31 Cumberland Road, Sale, Cheshire M33 3QT.

Lubbock Fine Chartered Accountants, Partner Anthony L. Sober, Russell Bedford House, City Forum, 250 City Road, London EC1V 2QQ. Tel: (071) 490 7766. Fax: (071) 490 5102.

Pancho Promotions, Director Sal Keegan, 'Pancho', 2 Chilgrove Avenue, Blackrod Village, Near Bolton, Greater Manchester BL6 5TR. Tel: (0204) 699454 (24hr answerphone). Mobile phone: (0836) 757834.

Touch of Class Costume Jewellery Specialists, Director Carol Fielding, 43 Balmoral Road, Accrington, Lancs BB5 6DB. Tel: (0254) 237302.

GOODS AND SERVICES

Abacus Colour Printers Ltd, Lowick House, Lowick, Near Ulverston, Cumbria LA12 8DX. Tel: (0229) 85 361/381. Fax: (0229) 85 348.

Baker Ross Ltd, Unit 53, Milmead Industrial Estate, Mill Mead Road, Tottenham, London N17 9QU. Tel: (081) 808 6948.

Building Society Choice, Riverside House, Rattlesden, Bury St Edmunds, Suffolk IP30 0SF. Tel: (0449) 736287. Fax: (0449) 737649.

Craft Creations Ltd, 1-7 Harpers Yard, Ruskin Road, Tottenham, London N17 8NE. Tel: (081) 885 2655. Fax: (081) 808 0746.

The Cutting Edge, Director Kevin McCarthy, Unit 14 CEC, Mill Lane, Coppull, Chorley, Lancs PR7 5AN. Tel: (0257) 792025.

Ethical Investment Research Service (EIRIS), 504 Bondway Business Centre, 71 Bondway, London SW8 1SQ. Tel: (071) 735 1351.

The Kite and Balloon Company, Managing Director Andrew V. Yeates, 613 Garratt Lane, London SW18 4SU. Tel: (081) 946 5962/5472.

Knaresborough Donkeys, Proprietor David W. Allott, 8 Park Place, Knaresborough, North Yorkshire HG5 0ER. Tel: (0423) 863641.

The Glenn Miller Orchestra (UK) Ltd, Director John Watson, 7 Lexington Way, Barnet, Herts EN5 2BN. Tel: (081) 440 4322. Fax: (081) 440 6446.

Peeks of Bournemouth, Riverside Lane, Tuckton, Bournemouth, Dorset BH6 3BR. Tel: (0202) 417777 (3 lines). Fax: (0202) 417729.

Recycling information

Save-A-Can, Elm House, 19 Elmshott Lane, Cippenham, Slough, Bucks SL1 5QS. Tel: (0628) 666658.

Steel Can Recycling Information Bureau, Kingsgate House, 536 Kings Road, London SW10 0TE. Tel: (071) 351 5208.

Recipes

SWEETS

Vanilla Fudge
(makes 1lb 2oz, about 500g)
You need: a 7-inch (18cm) square tin
      1lb 2oz (500g) granulated sugar
      3oz (75g) butter
      $3/4$ pint (150ml) evaporated milk
      $1/2$ teaspoon vanilla essence
      4 tablespoons milk

Oil the tin. Put all the ingredients into a large, heavy-based pan and stir over gentle heat until the sugar dissolves.

Boil for seven minutes. Take pan off the heat and test for setting: drop a little of the mixture into a cup of cold water, leave for a few seconds, then roll between finger and thumb. If it forms a soft ball, it's ready to beat. If not, boil for a little longer then test again.

Beat till thick and creamy. Pour into a tin. When the fudge is set but not hard, mark it into squares. Allow it to harden a little more then cut the squares and put them in paper sweet cases. (If you let the fudge get too hard before cutting, it will tend to break). Pack in foil-covered boxes.

Fruit fudge
(makes about $1^1/2$lb, 675g)
You need: a 7-inch square tin
      1lb (450g) granulated sugar
      4oz (100g) glacé cherries
      1 tablespoon golden syrup
      $1/2$ pint (200ml) evaporated milk
      2oz (50g) butter
      a few drops vanilla essence

149

Oil the tin. Cut the glacé cherries into quarters, rinse, dry well and set aside. Put all other ingredients into a large, heavy-based pan and finish as for Vanilla Fudge, adding the cherries *after* beating.

Chocolate fudge
(makes about 1lb 10oz, 725g)
You need: a 7-inch (18cm) square tin
          6oz (175g) plain chocolate
          1lb (450g) granulated sugar
          1/4 pint (150ml) milk
          4oz (100g) butter

Oil the tin. Break up the chocolate, put it into a large, heavy-based pan with all other ingredients. Stir over low heat until the chocolate melts and the sugar dissolves. Finish as for Vanilla Fudge.

Peppermint creams
(makes about 1 1/4lb, 575g)
You need: 1lb (450g) icing sugar, sieved
          1 small can sweetened condensed milk
          a few drops of peppermint essence
          edible green food colouring (use very sparingly)
          cornflour for dusting
          about 3oz (75g) melted chocolate

Blend the icing sugar and condensed milk till the mixture is smooth. Add essence to taste and just enough colouring to make the mixture a delicate pale green. (Don't drop the colouring straight from the bottle, but put one drop at a time into a teaspoon, so you're always in control of the degree of colour added.)

Roll out on a smooth surface lightly dusted with cornflour until about 1/4-inch (6mm) thick. Cut into shapes using a small round or square cutter. Cover loosely and leave in a cool place for 24 hours, until set. Dip some of the creams into melted chocolate, and allow to set on waxed paper (or a lightly greased baking tray).

Sugar animals
Use the same mixture as for peppermint creams, but vary the colours and flavours. Shape the fondant into animal shapes (mice, cats, rabbits, dogs, snakes). Use sweets and cake decorations for the features (strips of

angelica or liquorice make good tails), and leave to harden on waxed paper or a lightly greased baking tray.

Coconut ice
(needs no cooking, makes about 50 pieces)
You need: 18oz (500g) sieved icing sugar
          10 tablespoons sweetened condensed milk
          10oz (275g) desiccated coconut
          a few drops of pink or green food colouring

Mix the milk and sugar. Stir in the coconut and knead until well blended. Put half the mixture into a buttered tin. Add colour as desired to the remaining mixture and knead till well mixed in. Press this remaining mixture lightly on top of the mixture in the tin. Allow to set. Cut into 1-inch (2.5cm) squares.

The coconut ice will keep well for about three weeks if stored in an airtight tin with tissue between layers.

BISCUITS

Gingerbread men
(makes eight to ten)
You need: 10oz (275g) plain flour
          4oz (100g) caster sugar (use brown if you want a darker colour)
          4oz (100g) butter or margarine
          3 teaspoons ground ginger
          2^1/$_2$ tablespoons golden syrup
          small chocolate drop or currants

Preheat the oven to Mark 4, 350°F, 180°C. Cream the fat and sugar together until pale and fluffy. Warm the syrup, and add it with the dry ingredients to the fat and sugar mixture. Knead thoroughly, then roll out on a lightly floured surface until it's ^{3}/$_4$-inch (6mm) thick. Cut out with a gingerbread cutter and place the 'men' on a greased baking tray. Decorate with chocolate drops or currants for features. Bake till golden brown, usually about 15 minutes. Leave on the baking tray to cool a little before lifting on to a wire cooling tray. When fully cool, decorate with a narrow red ribbon round the necks.

Keeps for up to a week.

METRIC CONVERSION CHART

Dry measures

Ounces	Converted to the nearest unit of 25 grammes
1	25
2	50
3	75
4	100
5	150
6	175
7	200
8	225
9	250
10	275
11	300
12	350
13	375
14	400
15	425
16 (1lb)	450

Liquid measures

Imperial	Recommended ml
5 fluid oz ($^1/_4$ pint)	150
10 fluid oz ($^1/_2$ pint)	300
15 fluid oz ($^3/_4$ pint)	450
20 fluid oz (1 pint)	600
30 fluid oz (1$^1/_2$ pints)	900
45 fluid oz (1$^3/_4$ pints)	1000 (1 litre)

Index

Other books in this series

How to Start a Business from Home
Graham Jones
Second Edition

Most people have dreamed of starting their own business from home at some time or other; but how do you begin? What special skills do you need? This great value-for-money paperback has the answers, showing how you can profit from your own talents and experience, and start turning spare time into cash from the comfort of your own home. *How to Start a Business from Home* contains a wealth of ideas, projects, tips, facts, checklists and quick-reference information for everyone — whether in between jobs, taking early retirement, or students and others with time to invest. Packed with information on everything from choosing a good business idea and starting up to advertising, book-keeping and dealing with professionals, this book is essential reading for every budding entrepreneur. 'Full of ideas and advice.' *The Daily Mirror. Graham Jones BSc(Hons) is an editor, journalist and lecturer specialising in practical business subjects. His other books include Fit to Manage and The Business of Freelancing. 176pp, 1 85703 012 5.*

How to Do Your Own Advertising
Michael Bennie

'Entrepreneurs and small businesses are flooding the market with new products and services; the only way to beat the competition is successful selling — and that means advertising.' But what can you afford? This book is for anyone who needs — or wants — to advertise effectively, but does not want to pay agency rates. It will also be useful to those who simply want to know what is involved in advertising, whether as students, business people or interested laymen. What are the secrets of putting together effective ads? Even the basic design can be done by someone with a little imagination and creativity. This book shows you step-by-step how to assemble a simple, straightforward, yet highly successful ad or brochure with the minimum of outside help. Every step is clearly explained with the beginner in mind. There are numerous illustrations, lots of examples of actual ads, a variety of case studies to show the principles in practice and the aim throughout is to make advertising easy and enjoyable. Complete with questionnaires and checklists to help you check your progress. Michael Bennie has had many years' professional experience as a Sales Manager with a number of international companies, covering all aspects of sales and copywriting. He is now a freelance copywriter and advertising consultant, and Director of Studies at the Copywriting School. *176pp illus. 0 7463 0579 6.*

Other books in this series

How to Keep Business Accounts
Peter Taylor
Second Edition

A new revised edition of an easy-to-understand handbook for all business owners and managers. 'Will help you sort out the best way to carry out double entry book-keeping, as well as providing a clear step-by-step guide to accounting procedures.' *Mind Your Own Business.* 'Progresses through the steps to be taken to maintain an effective double entry book-keeping system with the minimum of bother.' *The Accounting Technician.* 'Compulsory reading.' *Manager, National Westminster Bank (Midlands).* Peter Taylor is a Fellow of the Institute of Chartered Accountants, and of the Chartered Association of Certified Accountants. He has many years' practical experience of advising small businesses.
176pp illus. 0 7463 0618 0.

How to Master Book-Keeping
An Introduction for Students
Peter Marshall

Book-keeping can seem a confusing subject for people coming to it for the first time. This very clear book will be welcomed by everyone wanting a really user-friendly guide to recording business transactions step-by-step. Illustrated at every stage with specimen entries, the book will also be an ideal companion for students taking LCCI, RSA, BTEC, accountancy technician and similar courses at schools, colleges or training centres. Typical business transactions are used to illustrate all the essential theory, practice and skills required to be effective in a real business setting. Contents: Preface, introduction, theory of double entry, day books, cash book, bank reconciliation, petty cash book, journal, postage book, the ledger, discounts, control accounts, trial balance, accruals and prepayments, revenue accounts, the balance sheet, manufacturing accounts, depreciation, bad and doubtful debts, partnership, limited companies, 'going limited', reflection, club accounts, asset disposals, correction of errors, VAT accounts. Peter Marshall BSc(Econ) BA(Hons) FRSA FSBT MBIM has been Tutor in Education at the University of Lancaster and Director of Studies at the Careers College, Cardiff. He has contributed regularly to *FOCUS on Business Education.*
192pp illus. 1 85703 022 2.

How to Master Business English
Michael Bennie

Are you communicating effectively? Do your business documents achieve the results you want? Or are they too often ignored or misunderstood? Good communication is the key to success in any business. Whether you are trying to sell a product, answer a query or complaint, or persuade colleagues, the way you express yourself is often as important as what you say. With lots of examples, checklists and questionnaires to help you, this book will speed you on your way, whether as manager, executive, or business student. Contents: Introduction, communication in business, planning, getting the right reaction, the writing process, layout, letters, memos, reports, construction, style, sales letters, letters of complaint, answering complaints, accounts queries, press releases, reports, filing, grammar, punctuation, spelling, glossary, answers to exercises. Michael Bennie is an English graduate with many years' practical experience of business communication both in government and industry. He is Director of Studies of the Department of Business Writing of Writers College, and author of *How to Do Your Own Advertising* in this series. *208pp illus. 07463 0582 6.*

How to Master Public Speaking
Anne Nicholls

Speaking well in public is one of the most useful skills any of us can acquire. People who can often become leaders in their business, profession or community, and the envy of their friends and colleagues. Whether you are a nervous novice or a practised pro, this step-by-step handbook tells you everything you need to know to master this highly prized communication skill. Contents: Preface, being a skilled communicator, preparation, researching your audience, preparing a speech, finding a voice, body language and non-verbal communication, dealing with nerves, audiovisual aids, the physical environment, putting it all together on the day, audience feedback, dealing with the media, glossary, further reading, useful contacts, index. Anne Hulbert Nicholls BA(Hons) PGCE was a Lecturer in Communications and Journalism in a College of Education for 14 years and ran courses in Presentation Skills and Effective Speaking for local business people. She now runs seminars and conferences for a publishing company and writes articles for a number of national magazines and newspapers. Her articles appear regularly in *Living* magazine. She has also worked in Public Relations and for BBC Radio. *160pp illus. 0 7463 0521 4.*

Other books in this series

How to Write a Report
John Bowden

Communicating effectively on paper is an essential skill for today's business or professional person. Good report-writing is a highly effective means of achieving a wide range of objectives, for example in managing an organisation, dealing with staffing, sales and marketing, production, computer operations, financial planning and reporting, feasibility studies and business innovation. Written by an experienced manager and staff trainer, this well-presented handbook provides a very clear step-by-step framework for every individual, whether dealing with professional colleagues, customers, clients, suppliers or junior or senior staff. Contents: Preparation and planning. Collecting and handling information. Writing the report: principles and techniques. Improving your thinking. Improving presentation. Achieving a good writing style. Making effective use of English. How to choose and use illustrations. Choosing paper, covers and binding. Appendices (examples, techniques, checklists), glossary, index. John Bowden BSc(Econ) MSc studied at the London School of Economics. He has long experience both as a professional manager in industry, and as a Senior Lecturer running courses in accountancy, auditing, and effective communication, up to senior management level. *160pp illus. 1 85703 035 4.*

How to Run a Local Campaign
Polly Bird

As people battle against vested interests for a better life, this book explains in a clear easy-to-read format the right approach to starting and winning a public campaign. Polly Bird, herself an experienced local campaigner, provides tips, advice and checklists from first steps and publicity through to funds, self-help options, and what to do on completion of a project. Including valuable campaigning address lists, this book is a must for everyone with a cause to fight. 'An excellent beginner's guide to successful campaigning.' *Green Magazine.* 'Contains everything the local activist needs to know.' *Dulwich Labour Party Newsletter.* 'Can help would-be campaign organisers to avoid many of the pitfalls and heartaches ahead.' *Conservative Newsline.* 'Polly Bird is someone that those in authority would be wise not to upset. Her book is a must for all who want to cause authority a headache. . .' *The Chemical Engineer.* *144pp illustrated. 0 7463 0539 7.*